# BLOCKCHAIN AND CRYPTOCURRENCIES

Edited by **Asma Salman**
and **Muthanna G. Abdul Razzaq**

**Blockchain and Cryptocurrencies**
http://dx.doi.org/10.5772/intechopen.74182
Edited by Asma Salman and Muthanna G. Abdul Razzaq

**Contributors**

Leonardo Jose Mataruna-Dos-Santos, Vanissa Wanick, Ireneusz Miciuła, Er'El Granot, Tatjana Boshkov, Alessandra Cretarola, Gianna Figà-Talamanca, Mike Cudd



First published in London, United Kingdom, 2019 by IntechOpen
IntechOpen is the global imprint of INTECHOPEN LIMITED, registered in England and Wales, registration number: 11086078, The Shard, 25th floor, 32 London Bridge Street
London, SE19SG – United Kingdom
Printed in Croatia

British Library Cataloguing-in-Publication Data
A catalogue record for this book is available from the British Library

Additional hard and PDF copies can be obtained from orders@intechopen.com

Blockchain and Cryptocurrencies , Edited by Asma Salman and Muthanna G. Abdul Razzaq
p. cm.
Print ISBN 978-1-78923-913-3
Online ISBN 978-1-83881-208-9
eBook (PDF) ISBN 978-1-78923-914-0

For EU product safety concerns:
IN TECH d.o.o., Prolaz Marije Krucifikse Kozulić 3, 51000 Rijeka, Croatia,
info@intechopen.com or visit our website at intechopen.com.

# Meet the editors

Dr. Asma Salman is an associate professor of finance, serving at the College of Business Administration at the American University in the Emirates. She completed her MBA in Finance and Accounting and earned a PhD in Finance from the School of Management at Harbin Institute of Technology, Harbin, China. With research credentials from Brunel Business School at Brunel University, London, she has been actively engaged in scientific research and has published credible articles in international journals and conferences. One of her recent publications on "Bitcoin" has gained wide visibility across the world and then went on to achieve the Blockchain Explorer certification from IBM. Dr. Salman also served as the Dubai cohort supervisor for students under the Nottingham Business School DBA program where she was affiliated as a visiting scholar for eight years. Her research has provided her with several awards and honors around the globe. Her research interests include accounting, international finance, blockchain, and digital currencies.

Professor Muthanna G. Abdul Razzaq completed his Bachelor Degree in Business Administration and Accounting from Al Mustansirya University. He attained his Postgraduate Diploma in Cost Accounting from Baghdad University, Iraq, and then moved to the UK to pursue his PhD in Management Accounting from the University of Manchester.

Starting his career with the Ministry of Irrigation, soon his passion for education compelled him to join Baghdad University. Going a step further, in 1997 Professor Muthanna joined as the Acting Chair of the Department of Accounting at Applied Science University, Jordan, and later in 1999 as the Deputy Dean of the Faculty of Business Administration at Ajman University of Science and Technology, United Arab Emirates. His constant drive to excel inspired him to establish the American University in the Emirates in 2006, where he also serves as the President and CEO.

During his career spanning four decades he has served in various roles as Chairman of the Academic Committee, Vice President for Scientific Research, Member of the Board of Governors, Vice Chancellor for Administrative and Financial Affairs, and Member of the Board of Trustees. An accountant by profession and a professor of accounting, Professor Muthanna is a visionary who carries with him a perfect blend of administrative and academic exposure, with equal grip on accounting-related subjects. A selfless initiator, Professor Muthanna, with a broad vision, is dedicated to devoting his life to the cause of education and educational reforms.

# Contents

# Preface

This book on blockchain and cryptocurrencies shows the alternative side of finance in the digital era. It is amazing to see how blockchain technology has disrupted different sectors and how the revolutionary payment mechanisms in the form of cryptocurrencies and exchanges are primarily witnessed in the financial sector. This is one of the true examples of moving from the "Internet of Use" to the "Internet of Value." Digital currencies have led the world to believe in an alternative economy. It includes both crypto and non-cryptocurrencies. Bitcoins, ethereum, altcoins, and the likes have captured the curiosity of economists, philosophers, venture capitalists, and financial gurus alike and has given a new kind of power to users, which is decentralized and anonymous, creating disruption in the financial markets. Currently, some countries have offered their own digital currencies as an alternative to fiat currencies, while others are recognizing digital currencies as an asset, a commodity, and so forth.

This book intends to feature the most talked about topic of cryptocurrencies along with its underlying technology of blockchain and how it has impacted the economy, the central banks, people, and organizations, and whether this power struggle of sorts will venture into a new digitized economy. It is divided into four main sections, with topics on Bitcoin, blockchain and digital returns, the impact of cryptocurrencies in gaming, and cryptocurrency exchanges. This book shows many different aspects of the treatment of cryptocurrencies in various parts of the world along with the technology that underpins it, the blockchain. The diversity of the authors who sum up this book signify the importance, acceptance, and implementation of this alternative currency and payment mechanism.

The first section is titled "Bitcoin." Authors Alessandra Cretarola and Gianna Figà-Talamanca from Italy present recent developments in Bitcoin price modeling and related applications. They investigate the relation between the correlation parameter and possible bubble effects in the asset price. The authors then use a multivariate framework to represent the special feature of Bitcoin being traded on several exchanges and discuss conditions to rule out arbitrage opportunities in this setting.

Section 2 deals with the "Blockchain and Digital Returns" and two chapters form part of this section. Tatjana Boshkov from Macedonia aims to provide an analysis of the use of cryptocurrencies in general, especially Bitcoin as the technology adoption in the presence of network externalities. The chapter explores financial privacy, which is a very sensitive issue that uses digital currency (or cryptocurrency) and discusses private choices versus political rules. Authors Mike Cudd, Kristen Ritterbush, Marcelo Eduardo, and Chris Smith from the United States discuss profiling the risk and return metrics of cryptocurrencies. The cryptocurrency returns over different observation periods are examined and compared to those of conventional currencies and equities for relevance and proportion.

Section 3 covers the "Impact of Cryptocurrencies in Gaming" where Leonardo José Mataruna-dos- Santos from the United Arab Emirates and Vanissa Wanick from the United Kingdom explore the cryptocurrencies in ludic economies where games have been described as having their own economic models. The authors give an overview of the current state of the art economic models within games and eSports. This aims to situate and analyze the application of these business models derived from games, eSports, and the future of ludic economies.

Section 4 deals with "Cryptocurrency Exchanges" and two chapters also form part of this section.

Author Er'el Granot from Israel explains why Bitcoin and other cryptocurrencies have received a lot of criticism during the last nine years. The author then analyzes the origin of the value of Bitcoin and other cryptocoins from the perspective of the Austrian School of Economics. It is explained that Bitcoin does not contradict the regression theorem. First, because the initial value estimation can be a random event, and second, the Bitcoin network (even now) has a non-monetary value.

Author Ireneusz Miciuła from Poland explores the global development of cryptocurrencies and discusses the functioning of a financial system based on cryptocurrencies and its significance for economies. The author presents the development of the global cryptocurrency market and analyzes the history of the most popular cryptocurrency, the Bitcoin. This last chapter ends the book on a rather high note of how a proper financial system through cryptocurrencies can be implemented in economies.

Last, but certainly not the least, the successful completion of this book has been the result of various "behind-the-scene" members who have supported it right from its inception until the publication process. We would like to express our sincere gratitude to all the authors for their diverse contributions. Also, thanks go to Author Service Manager Ms. Romina Skomersic for her endless support during the publishing process.

**Dr. Asma Salman**
Associate Professor of Finance
College of Business Administration
American University in the Emirates
United Arab Emirates

**Professor Muthanna G. Abdul Razzaq**
President and CEO
American University in the Emirates
United Arab Emirates

Section 1

# Bitcoin

Chapter 1

# Modeling Bitcoin Price and Bubbles

Alessandra Cretarola and Gianna Figà-Talamanca

Additional information is available at the end of the chapter

http://dx.doi.org/10.5772/intechopen.79386

**Abstract**

The goal of this chapter is to present recent developments about Bitcoin[1] price modeling and related applications. Precisely, we consider a bivariate model in continuous time to describe the behavior of Bitcoin price and of the investors' attention on the overall network. The attention index affects Bitcoin price through a suitable dependence on the drift and diffusion coefficients and a possible correlation between the sources of randomness represented by the driving Brownian motions. The model is fitted on historical data of Bitcoin prices, by considering the total trading volume and the Google *Search Volume Index* as proxies for the attention measure. Moreover, a closed formula is computed for European-style derivatives on Bitcoin. Finally, we discuss two possible extensions of the model. Precisely, we investigate the relation between the correlation parameter and possible bubble effects in the asset price; further, we consider a multivariate framework to represent the special feature of Bitcoin being traded on several exchanges and we discuss conditions to rule out arbitrage opportunities in this setting.

**Keywords:** Bitcoin, market attention, arbitrage, option pricing, bubbles

## 1. Introduction

Bitcoin is a digital currency built on a peer-to-peer network and on the blockchain, a public ledger where all transactions are recorded and made available to all nodes. Opposite to traditional banking transactions, based on trust for counterparty, Bitcoin relies on cryptography and on a consensus protocol for the network. The entire system is founded on an open source software created in 2009 by a computer scientist known under the pseudonym Satoshi Nakamoto, whose identity is still unknown (see [1]). Hence, Bitcoin is an independent digital

[1]We use the following rule throughout the paper: the term BitCoin refers to the whole system network while Bitcoin refers to the digital currency.

currency, not subject to the control of central authorities and without inflation; furthermore, transactions in the network are pseudonymous and irreversible.

Bitcoin and the underlying blockchain technology have gained much attention in the last few years. Research on Bitcoin often deals with cybersecurity and legitimacy issues such as the analysis of double spending possibilities and other cyber-threats; recently, high returns and volatility have attracted research toward the analysis of Bitcoin price efficiency as well as its dynamics (see, among others, [2–4]). Moreover, many contributions claim that Bitcoin price is driven by attention or sentiment about the Bitcoin system itself; see [5–8]. Possible driving factors for the sentiment about the Bitcoin system are the volume of Google searches or Wikipedia requests as in [5], or more traditional indicators as the number or volume of transactions, as suggested in [6]. In [9], the author suggests a time series model in order to identify the dynamic relation between speculation activity and price.

In this chapter, after having introduced the basic concepts underlying Bitcoin, we sum up and describe to a broader audience the recent outcomes of the research reported in [10], by avoiding unnecessary technicalities. Some new insights are also given by looking at possible extensions in order to take into account the presence of bubble effects or the special feature of Bitcoin being traded in different online platforms (exchanges) that will be further investigated in our future research.

## 2. The Bitcoin network

We recall that Bitcoin was first introduced as an electronic payment system between peers by Satoshi Nakamoto (pseudonym) in [1]. Opposite to traditional transactions, which are based on the trust in financial intermediaries, this system relies on the network, on the fixed rules and on cryptography. Bitcoins can be purchased on appropriate websites that allow to change usual currencies in the cryptocurrency.

The Bitcoin network has several attractive properties for its users:

- No central bank authority for money supply and no regulator;
- Transactions are 24/7 and without any country border;
- Transaction cost are almost negligible with respect to traded amount;
- Transaction are anonymous;
- The security of each transaction is guaranteed by cryptography and digital signature;
- The security of the whole network is guaranteed by construction unless more than 50% of the network nodes agree on a deceptive action.

As a digital payment system, Bitcoins may be used to pay for several online services and goods. Special applications have been designed for smartphones and tablets for transactions in Bitcoins and some ATMs have appeared all over the world (see Coin ATM radar) to change traditional currencies in Bitcoins. Accepting Bitcoins as a payment method is also related to an advertisement opportunity for companies. However, the high returns achieved in the last few years have transformed Bitcoin in a speculative asset affecting its use as a form of payment.

The Bitcoin system has been subject to many cracks but has proven to be very resilient as the value of the cryptocurrency was able to rise again after all the falls. Nevertheless, at the time of writing, Bitcoin was experiencing a fall in its exchange rate with main fiat currencies.

Two of the main crackdowns were China enforcement in December 2013 and Mt. Gox bankruptcy in February 2014.

Besides technical and regulation issues, the Bitcoin system also faces reputational concerns.

In fact, the ambiguity of anonymous transactions has blamed the network of allowing several criminal activities such as buying illegal goods, money laundering or the financing of terrorism actions. As a representative example, we recall that *The Silk Road* was a website that started selling narcotics and illegal drugs in 2011, payable in Bitcoins. The website was finally shutdown by 2013 and the owner was arrested and sentenced to life in prison. Again, anonymous transactions make it possible to use huge quantities of money, exchanged in Bitcoins, without declaring its origin, hence allowing for possible money laundering. However, according to a research performed by the UK government, the highest score related to money laundering is still cash, followed by the bank, accountancy and legal service providers (see https://www.gov.uk/government/publications/uk-national-risk-assessment-of-money-laundering-and-terrorist-financing).

It is worth noticing that while counterparties are represented by secret addresses and are anonymous, all transactions are recorded and might be traced. Investigation is hence favored by this feature of the network.

Despite the flaws in the system, Bitcoin has achieved a notwithstanding rise in recent years.

In **Figure 1**, we report Bitcoin price and returns from January 2012 to December 2017 (source https://blockchain.info/en/charts).

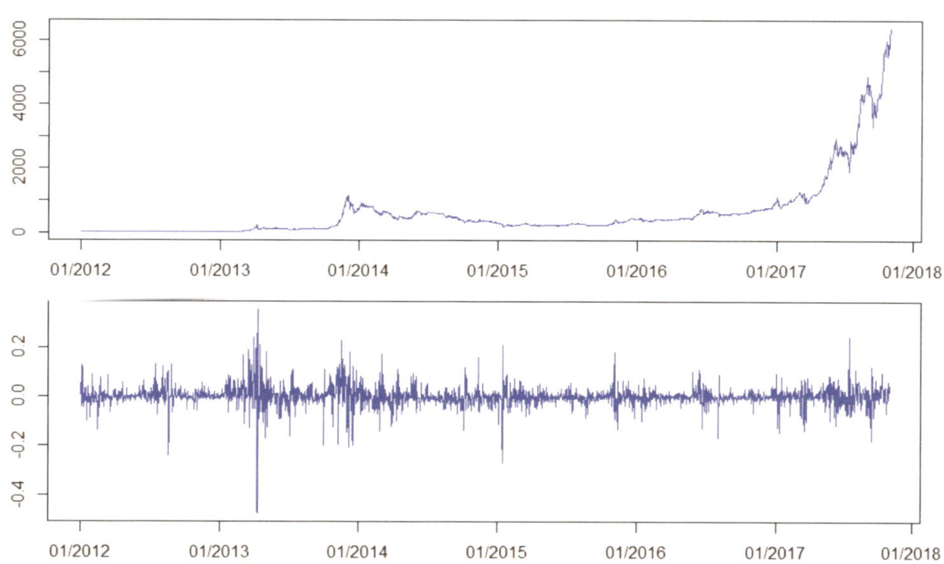


**Figure 1.** Bitcoin price (top) and returns (bottom) from January 2012 to December 2017.

## 3. An attention-based model

The model we suggest in what follows is motivated by findings in [5, 6, 8, 11] where it is showed that Bitcoin price is related to investors' attention measured by the trading volume and/or the number of searches in engines such as Google and Wikipedia. Bitcoin is treated as a financial stock as suggested in [12] and the suggested model may be applied in principle to other assets that are proven to depend on market attention.

### 3.1. The model specification

Consider a probability space $(\Omega, \mathcal{F}, P)$ endowed with a filtration $\mathbb{F} = \{\mathcal{F}_t, t \geq 0\}$ satisfying usual assumptions of right continuity and completeness.

Let us denote the Bitcoin price process as $S = \{S_t, t \geq 0\}$ and assume that it depends on an attention factor denoted by $A = \{A_t, t \geq 0\}$. The dynamics of the two processes are described by the following equation:

$$\begin{cases} \dfrac{dS_t}{S_t} = \mu_S A_t dt + \sigma_S \sqrt{A_t} dW_t, \, S_0 = s_0 \in \mathbb{R}^+ \\ dA_t = \mu_A A_t dt + \sigma_A A_t dZ_t, \, A_0 = a_0 \in \mathbb{R}^+, \end{cases} \tag{1}$$

where $\mu_A, \mu_S, \sigma_A > 0, \sigma_S > 0$ are constant parameters and $(W, Z) = \{(W_t, Z_t), t \geq 0\}$ is an $(\mathbb{F}, P)$-standard Brownian motion in $\mathbb{R}^2$. Assume that $\mathcal{F}_t = \sigma(W_u, Z_u, u \leq t)$, for each $t \geq 0$.

It is well known that the above dynamics for the attention factor is a geometric Brownian motion, the solution of which is given by $A_t = A_0 \exp\left(\left(\mu_A - \frac{\sigma_A^2}{2}\right)t + \sigma_A Z_t\right)$ for $t \geq 0$ which has a log-normal distribution; integrating the price process is straightforward to get

$$S_t = S_0 \exp\left(\left(\mu_S - \frac{\sigma_S^2}{2}\right)\int_0^t A_u du + \sigma_S \int_0^t \sqrt{A_u} dW_u\right), t \geq 0. \tag{2}$$

### 3.2. Statistical properties and model fitting

We collect in this subsection the properties of the logarithmic returns obtained by the price process defined in Eq. (1).

Consider the discrete process $\{(A_{i\Delta}, S_{i\Delta}), i = 1, 2, \ldots, n\}$ obtained by sampling the price process and the attention factor at times $t_i = i\Delta, i = 1, 2, \ldots n$ with constant observation step $\Delta$; denote the logarithmic changes of the process by $R_i = \log \frac{S_{i\Delta}}{S_{(i-1)\Delta}}, P_i = \log \frac{A_{i\Delta}}{A_{(i-1)\Delta}}$ and define $X_i := \int_{(i-1)\Delta}^{i\Delta} A_u du$.

Note that $R_i, i = 1, 2, \ldots n$ represent the logarithmic returns of asset S for the sampling dates and that $X_i, i = 1, 2, \ldots n$ the cumulative attention in the time interval $[(i-1)\Delta, i\Delta]$. Then it is straightforward to prove the following:

Theorem 2.1. *The random vector* $\mathbf{R} = (R_1, R_2, \ldots R_n)$*, given* $\mathbf{X} = (X_1, X_2, \ldots X_n)$*, is normally distributed with mean* $\mathbf{m}$ *and covariance matrix* $\Sigma$ *where*

$$m_i = \left(\mu_S - \frac{{\sigma_S}^2}{2}\right) X_i, \quad \text{for } i = 1, 2, \ldots n, \qquad (3)$$

$$\Sigma = Diag\left({\sigma_S}^2 X_1, {\sigma_S}^2 X_2, .., {\sigma_S}^2 X_n\right).$$

*Proof.* In order to prove the theorem it suffices to remind that, for i = 1, 2, …, n, the random variable $\int_{(i-1)\Delta}^{i\Delta} \sqrt{A_u} dW_u$, conditional on knowing $X_i$, is normally distributed with zero mean and variance $X_i$, and that the increments of the Brownian motion $W$ are independent.

As for the unconditional distribution, it is easy to obtain, for $i = 1, 2, \ldots, n$,

$$E[R_i] = \left(\mu_S - \frac{{\sigma_S}^2}{2}\right) E[X_i], \qquad (4)$$

$$Var[R_i] = \left(\mu_S - \frac{{\sigma_S}^2}{2}\right)^2 Var[X_i] + {\sigma_S}^2 E[X_i],$$

where $E[X_i]$, $Var[X_i]$ can be computed in closed form as a function of $\mu_A, \sigma_A, \Delta$ (see for example [10]). The above outcomes are applied in order to derive the likelihood of the vector $(\mathbf{R}, \mathbf{X})$. Indeed, by simply applying Bayes' rule, we get the following result:

Proposition 2.2. The joint probability density of the vector $(\mathbf{R}, \mathbf{X})$ is given by $g : \mathbb{R} \times \mathbb{R}^+ \to \mathbb{R}$ with

$$g(r, x) = f_{X_1}(x_1) \prod_{i=2}^{n} f_{X_i|X_{i-1}}(x_i) \prod_{i=1}^{n} \frac{1}{\sqrt{2\pi\sigma_S^2 x_i}} \exp\left\{ -\frac{r_i - \left(\mu_S - \frac{\sigma_S^2}{2}\right) x_i}{2\sigma_S^2 x_i} \right\}, \qquad (5)$$

where $f_{X_1}(\cdot)$ and $f_{X_i|X_{i-1}}(\cdot)$ are the probability density function of $X_1$ and $X_i$ given $X_{i-1}$, respectively.

The proof follows from Bayes' rule and application of Theorem 2.1.

It is worth to remark that the probability density $g(\cdot)$ in Eq. (5) depends on suitable choices for $f_{X_1}(\cdot)$ and $f_{X_i|X_{i-1}}(\cdot)$. Under our assumptions, such densities are not given within known distribution; however, by applying outcomes in [13], we can approximate them as log-normals with means and variances given as closed expressions of $(\mu_A, \sigma_A)$.

Precisely, we have that $f_{X_1}(\cdot) = LN(\alpha, \nu)$ and, for $i = 2, 3, \ldots n, f_{X_i|X_{i-1}}(\cdot) = LN(\alpha_i, \nu_i)$, with

$$\alpha_1 = \log\left(\frac{\mathbb{E}[X_1]^2}{\sqrt{\mathbb{E}\left[{X_1}^2\right]}}\right), \quad \nu_1^2 = \log\left(\frac{\mathbb{E}\left[{X_1}^2\right]}{\mathbb{E}[X_1]^2}\right), \qquad (6)$$

$$\alpha_i = \log(X_{i-1}) + \left(\mu_A - \frac{\sigma_A^2}{2}\right)\Delta, \quad \nu_i^2 = \sigma_A^2 \Delta.$$

We apply the outcomes above in order to estimate model parameters according to the maximum-likelihood method (see for example [14, 15]) where the likelihood is approximated by applying the Levy approximation [13].

Parameter estimates are obtained as

$$\left(\widehat{\mu}_A, \widehat{\mu}_S, \widehat{\sigma}_A, \widehat{\sigma}_S\right) = \operatorname{argmax}_{\mu_A, \mu_S, \sigma_A, \sigma_S} \log\ell\left(\mu_A, \mu_S, \sigma_A, \sigma_S; \boldsymbol{r}, \boldsymbol{x}\right), \tag{7}$$

where

$$\begin{aligned} \log\ell\left(\mu_A, \mu_S, \sigma_A, \sigma_S; \boldsymbol{r}, \boldsymbol{x}\right) = & \sum_{i=1}^{n} \log \frac{1}{\sqrt{2\pi x_i \sigma_S^2}} - \frac{\left(r_i - \left(\mu_S - \frac{\sigma_S^2}{2}\right) x_i\right)^2}{2x_i {\sigma^2}_S} \\ & + \sum_{i=1}^{n} \log \frac{1}{x_i \sqrt{2\pi {v_i}^2}} - \frac{\left(\log x_i - \alpha_i\right)^2}{2{v_i}^2} \end{aligned} \tag{8}$$

### 3.3. Empirical application on Bitcoin prices

The first step in our procedure is to identify possible measures of investors' attention. As already mentioned in the introduction, we consider the total trading volume on Bitcoin available from https://blockchain.info as well as the search volume index (SVI) for Google searches on the topic "bitcoin" provided by https://trends.google.it/trends/.

The trading volume of exchange is a classical measure of the attractiveness of a traded asset for an investor; besides, in [16], the authors find evidence that the latter captures the attention of retail/uniformed investors.

We consider daily data from January 1, 2015, to June 30, 2017, for the total volume and the SVI Index. As for the daily value of the Bitcoin, we have considered the average mean across main exchanges represented by the Index in https://blockchain.info.

In **Table 1**, the outcomes for parameter estimates, obtained by maximizing the approximate likelihood given the observed time series, are summed up.

| | $\widehat{\mu}_A$ | $\widehat{\sigma}_A$ | $\widehat{\mu}_S$ | $\widehat{\sigma}_S$ |
|---|---|---|---|---|
| *A* = *Vol* | 0.9571 | 1.1346 | 0.0218 | 0.0829 |
| *A* = *SVI* | 1.3584 | 1.0687 | 0.0743 | 0.1559 |

**Table 1.** Parameter estimates for the model in Eq. (1) fitted on daily observations from January 2015 to June 2017.

## 4. A closed formula for Bitcoin option prices

In this section, we show how to characterize the price of European call options on Bitcoins in the underlying market model. Let us fix a finite time horizon $T > 0$ and assume the existence of a riskless asset (also called the savings account), whose price process $B = \{B_t, t \in [0,T]\}$ is given by

$$B_t = \exp\left(\int_0^t r(s)ds\right), \quad t \in [0,T], \tag{9}$$

where $r : [0,T] \to \mathbb{R}$ is a bounded, deterministic function representing the instantaneous risk-free interest rate. To be reasonable, the market model must avoid arbitrage opportunities, that is, investment strategies that do not require an initial investment and that do not expose to any risk and lead to a positive value with positive probability. From a mathematical point of view, this means to check that the set of equivalent martingale measures for the Bitcoin price process $S$ is nonempty. Precisely, it is possible to prove that it contains more than a single element.

**Lemma 3.1.** *Every equivalent martingale measure $Q$ for $S$ is characterized by its density process with respect to the initial probability measure $P$ as follows:*

$$\left.\frac{dQ}{dP}\right|_{\mathcal{F}_t} = \exp\left(-\int_0^t \frac{\mu_S A_u - r(u)}{\sigma_S\sqrt{A_u}} dW_u - \int_0^t \gamma_u dZ_u - \frac{1}{2}\int_0^t \left(\frac{\mu_S A_u - r(u)}{\sigma_S\sqrt{A_u}}\right)^2 du - \frac{1}{2}\int_0^t {\gamma_u}^2 du\right), \tag{10}$$

*where $\gamma = \{\gamma_t, t \in [0,T]\}$ is an $\mathbb{F}$-adapted process such that $\int_0^T {\gamma_u}^2 du < +\infty$, $P$-a.s.*

The proof can be deduced from that of Lemma 1.4 in [10], where they also account for a possible delay between the attention factor and its effect on Bitcoin prices trend. The process $\gamma$ can be interpreted as the risk perception associated to the future direction or future possible movements of the Bitcoin market. Since $S$ is the only tradable asset, the risk perception is not fixed and this explains the nonuniqueness of the martingale measure $Q$ in this market framework that turns out to be incomplete. Consequently, given any European-type contingent claim, it is not possible in general to find a self-financing strategy whose terminal value exactly replicates the payoff of the claim. We recall that the notion of completeness is related to the uniqueness of the martingale measure. Indeed, in complete markets, the no-arbitrage price of any derivative is uniquely determined by the unique martingale measure. On the other hand, in incomplete markets, we deal with a family of martingale measures and have at our disposal a set of possible prices, which are all compatible with the "no-arbitrage condition." One common approach to option pricing in incomplete markets in the mathematical financial literature is to select one specific martingale measure (which can be also called *pricing measure*) under which the discounted traded assets are martingales and to compute option prices via expectation under this measure via risk-neutral evaluation formulas. One simple example of a candidate equivalent martingale measure is the so-called *minimal martingale measure* (see [17, 18]), which minimizes the relative entropy, of the objective measure $P$, with respect to any risk-neutral measure. In this setting, its economic interpretation is that agents do not wish to be compensated for the risk associated with the fluctuations of the stochastic attention factor, which corresponds to the hypothesis of [19] in the stochastic volatility framework. This is the probability measure which corresponds to the choice $\gamma \equiv 0$ in Eq. (10). Intuitively, under the minimal martingale measure, say $\widehat{P}$, the drift of the Brownian motion driving the Bitcoin price process is modified to make $S$ an $\mathbb{F}$-martingale, while the drift of the Brownian motion which is strongly orthogonal to $S$ is not affected by the change measure from $P$ to $\widehat{P}$. More precisely, by Girsanov's theorem, the $\mathbb{R}^2$-valued process $\left(\widehat{W},\widehat{Z}\right)=\left\{\left(\widehat{W}_t,\widehat{Z}_t\right),t\in[0,T]\right\}$ defined by

$$\widehat{W}_t := W_t + \int_0^t \frac{\mu_S A_u - r(u)}{\sigma_S\sqrt{A_u}}du, \quad \widehat{Z}_t := Z_t, \tag{11}$$

is an $\left(\mathbb{F},\widehat{P}\right)$-standard Brownian motion. Under any equivalent martingale measure, the discounted Bitcoin price process $\tilde{S}=\left\{\tilde{S}_t,t\in[0,T]\right\}$ given by $\tilde{S}_t:=\frac{S_t}{B_t}$, for each $t\in[0,T]$ behaves like a martingale. Precisely, on the probability space $\left(\Omega,\mathcal{F},\widehat{P}\right)$, the pair $(\tilde{S},A)$ has the following dynamics:

$$\begin{cases} d\tilde{S}_t = \sigma_S\sqrt{A_t}\tilde{S}_t d\widehat{W}_t, \ \tilde{S}_0 = s_0 \in \mathbb{R}^+, \\ dA_t = \mu_A A_t dt + \sigma_A A_t dZ_t, \ A_0 = a_0 \in \mathbb{R}^+. \end{cases} \tag{12}$$

Equivalently, we can write the discounted Bitcoin price process $\tilde{S}$ as

$$\tilde{S}_t = s_0 \exp\left(\sigma_S\int_0^t\sqrt{A_u}d\widehat{W}_u - \frac{\sigma_S^2}{2}\int_0^t A_u du\right), \quad t\in[0,T]. \tag{13}$$

Clearly, under the minimal martingale measure $\widehat{P}$, the Bitcoin price process $S$ satisfies

$$dS_t = r(t)S_t dt + \sigma_S\sqrt{A_t}S_t d\widehat{W}_t, \quad S_0 = s_0 \in \mathbb{R}^+, \tag{14}$$

where $r(t)$ is the risk-free interest rate at time $t$.

**Remark 3.2.** *Note that, under any equivalent martingale measure that keeps the drift of the attention factor dynamics linear in A (in particular, under the minimal martingale measure), the model proposed in* [10] *nests the Hull-White stochastic volatility model, which corresponds to the particular case where* $\sigma_S=1$; *see* [19]. *Indeed, the authors only referred to a risk-neutral framework without describing the dynamics under the physical measure and consequently characterizing the existence of any equivalent martingale measure.*

Now, we compute the fair price of a Bitcoin European call option via the risk-neutral evaluation approach, so it can be expressed as expected value of the terminal payoff under the selected pricing measure, that is, the minimal martingale measure. Let $C_T=(S_T-K)^+$ be the $\mathcal{F}_T$-measurable random variable representing the payoff of a European call option on the Bitcoin with price $S$ with date of maturity $T$ and strike price $K$, which can be traded on the underlying digital market. Recall that $X_{t,T}=X_T-X_t$, for each $t\in[0,T)$, refers to the variation of the integrated attention process $X$ defined over the interval $[t,T]$. Then, denote by $E\widehat{P}[\cdot|\mathcal{F}_t]$ the conditional expectation with respect to the $\sigma$-field $\mathcal{F}_t$ under the probability measure $\widehat{P}$ and so on. Define the function $C^{BS}:[0,T)\times\mathbb{R}^+\times\mathbb{R}^+\to\mathbb{R}$ as follows:

$$C^{BS}(t,s,x) := s\mathcal{N}(d_1(t,s,x)) - Ke^{-\int_0^t r(u)du}\mathcal{N}(d_2(t,s,x)), \tag{15}$$

where

$$d_1(t,s,x) = \frac{\log\left(\frac{s}{K}\right) + \int_0^t r(u)du + \frac{\sigma_S^2}{2}x}{\sigma_S\sqrt{x}} \tag{16}$$

and $d_2(t,s,x) = d_1(t,s,x) - \sigma_S\sqrt{x}$, or more explicitly

$$d_2(t,s,x) = \frac{\log\left(\frac{s}{K}\right) + \int_0^t r(u)du - \frac{\sigma_S^2}{2}x}{\sigma_S\sqrt{x}}. \tag{17}$$

Here, $\mathcal{N}$ stands for the standard Gaussian cumulative distribution function, that is,

$$\mathcal{N}(y) = \frac{1}{\sqrt{2\pi}}\int_{-\infty}^{y} e^{-\frac{z^2}{2}}dz, \quad \forall\ y \in \mathbb{R}. \tag{18}$$

The following result provides the risk-neutral price of the option under the minimal martingale measure $\widehat{P}$. The proof is straightforward and may be derived by using similar arguments to those developed in [19].

**Proposition 3.3**. *The risk-neutral price $C_t$ at time t of a European call option written on the Bitcoin with price S expiring in T and with strike price K is given by the formula*

$$\begin{aligned} C_t &= E^{\widehat{P}}\left[C^{BS}(t,S_t,X_{t,T})|S_t\right] \\ &= S_t\int_0^{+\infty}\mathcal{N}(d_1(t,S_t,x))f_{X_{t,T}}(x)dx - Ke^{-\int_t^T r(u)du}\int_0^{+\infty}\mathcal{N}(d_2(t,S_t,x))f_{X_{t,T}}(x)dx, \end{aligned} \tag{19}$$

*where the function $C^{BS}$ is defined in Eq.* (15)*; the functions $d_1(\cdot)$, $d_2(\cdot)$ are, respectively, given in Eqs.* (16)-(17)*; and $f_{X_{t,T}}(\cdot)$ denotes the density function of $X_{t,T}$, for each $t \in [0,T)$, provided that it exists.*

Hence, the resulting risk-neutral pricing formula when evaluated in $S_t$ corresponds to the expected value of Black & Scholes price as defined in [20] at time $t \in [0,T)$ of a European call option written on $S$, with strike price $K$ and maturity $T$, in a financial market where the volatility is random and given by $\sigma_S\sqrt{\frac{X_{t,T}}{T-t}}$.

### 4.1. A numerical application

In order to appreciate the performance of the pricing formula in Eq. (19), we compute model prices for option traded on the online platform http://www.deribit.com on July, 30, 2017, by plugging in the estimated parameters. The outcomes are compared with the Black & Scholes benchmark (see [20]) as a reference price, computed by plugging the volatility parameter estimated on the same time series of the trading volume/SVI index, and with the bid-ask prices provided in the website. Best overall pricing values are obtained when market attention is

| T-K | Market bid | Market ask | Model volume | Model Google SVI | Benchmark BS |
|---|---|---|---|---|---|
| Aug-2200 | 0.1662 | 0.2318 | 0.2029 | 0.2282 | 0.1967 |
| Aug-2300 | 0.1670 | 0.2072 | 0.1737 | 0.2032 | 0.1655 |
| Aug-2400 | 0.1390 | 0.1845 | 0.1469 | 0.1802 | 0.1369 |
| Aug-2500 | 0.1142 | 0.1638 | 0.1228 | 0.1591 | 0.1112 |
| Aug-2600 | 0.0922 | 0.1376 | 0.1014 | 0.1399 | 0.0887 |
| Aug-2700 | 0.0749 | 0.1202 | 0.0828 | 0.1226 | 0.0695 |
| Aug-2800 | 0.0572 | 0.1047 | 0.0684 | 0.107 | 0.0535 |
| Aug-2900 | 0.0442 | 0.0983 | 0.0549 | 0.0931 | 0.0405 |
| Sept-2200 | 0.1991 | 0.2648 | 0.2546 | 0.3204 | 0.2173 |
| Sept-2300 | 0.1766 | 0.2432 | 0.2321 | 0.3019 | 0.1906 |
| Sept-2400 | 0.1890 | 0.2230 | 0.2113 | 0.2844 | 0.1662 |
| Sept-2500 | 0.1375 | 0.2042 | 0.1919 | 0.2679 | 0.1439 |
| Sept-2600 | 0.1207 | 0.1828 | 0.1741 | 0.2523 | 0.1239 |
| Sept-2700 | 0.1120 | 0.1668 | 0.1576 | 0.2377 | 0.1060 |
| Sept-2800 | 0.0953 | 0.1504 | 0.1463 | 0.2239 | 0.0903 |
| Sept-2900 | 0.0848 | 0.1422 | 0.1325 | 0.2109 | 0.0764 |

**Table 2.** Comparison between model prices computed according to formula in Eq. (19), Black & Scholes formula in [20], and the bid and ask prices provided in http:\\www.deribit.comfor options traded on July, 30, 2017, and expiring on August 25, 2017, and on September 28, 2017.

measured by volume; in the case of the SVI Google index, near-term options are very close to the mid-value of the bid-ask, while next-term options are overpriced. One possible explanation is that investors that get information about Bitcoin on search engines are more likely to be uninformed/retail investors that are self-exciting and may add spurious noise to the Bitcoin price volatility leading to an increase in call option prices (**Table 2**).

## 5. The presence of model stock bubbles

Motivated by empirical evidences (see for example [21, 22]), we discuss a generalization of the model introduced in Section 3.1, which is capable to describe speculative bubbles in Bitcoin markets.

Precisely, we fix a finite time horizon $T > 0$ and assume that the underlying Brownian motions $W$ and $Z$ are correlated with constant correlation coefficient $\rho \in (-1, 1)$, that is, $< W, Z>_t = \rho t$ for each $t \in [0, T]$. If $V = \{V_t, t \in [0, T]\}$ is an additional $(\mathbb{F}, P)$-Brownian motion that is $P$-independent of $Z$, then we can write

$$W_t = \rho Z_t + \sqrt{1-\rho^2} V_t, \quad t \in [0,T]. \tag{20}$$

Without loss of generality, we assume that the interest rate is fixed and equal to zero. In this setting, the discounted Bitcoin price trend and the market attention factor dynamics are described by

$$\begin{cases} dS_t = \mu_S A_t S_t dt + \sigma_S \sqrt{A_t} S_t (\rho dZ_t + \overline{\rho} dV_t), & S_0 = s_0 \in \mathbb{R}^+, \\ dA_t = \mu_A A_t dt + \sigma_A A_t dZ_t, & A_0 = a_0 \in \mathbb{R}^+, \end{cases} \tag{21}$$

where we have set $\overline{\rho} := \sqrt{1-\rho^2}$. The aim is to investigate the existence of asset-price bubbles in the underlying Bitcoin market model.

By simulating trajectories for the asset price $S$ according to the model in Eq. (1) for several values of the correlation parameter, it seems that the latter is related to the presence of bubble effect; in fact, in **Figure 2**, we plot examples of trajectories for $\rho = 0, -0.5, 0.5, 1$, respectively where higher positive values for the correlation appear to boost the asset value.

Indeed, we will show formally that the possibility of Bitcoin speculative bubbles is related to the sign of the correlation parameter $\rho$.

The mathematical theory of financial bubbles is developed, among others, in [23–25]. Precisely, we introduce the following definition from [23].

**Definition 4.1.** *The Bitcoin price process $S$ has a bubble on the time interval $[0,T]$ if $S$ is a strict $\mathbb{F}$-local martingale under the chosen risk-neutral measure.*

The term strict $\mathbb{F}$-local martingale refers to the fact that $S$ is an $\mathbb{F}$-local martingale, but not a true $\mathbb{F}$-martingale under the chosen risk-neutral measure. Further, since $S$ is nonnegative, we must have that $S$ is an $\mathbb{F}$-supermartingale (we refer to [26] for rigorous definitions and related concepts).

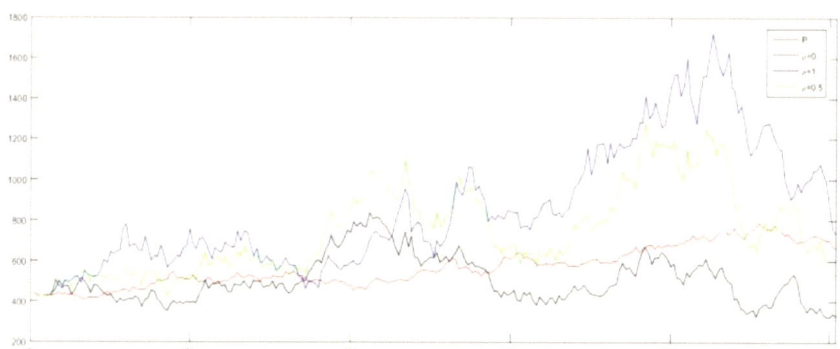


**Figure 2.** Simulated trajectories with $n$ = 250 daily observations for the attention process (red) and the corresponding Bitcoin price dynamics for $\rho = 0$ (black), $\rho = 0.5$(green), and $\rho = 1$ (blue).

Recall that the absence of arbitrage opportunities is "essentially" equivalent to the existence of a probability measure $Q$, equivalent to the initial probability $P$, under which the discounted price process satisfies the martingale property.

**Remark 4.2.** *Note that stock bubbles arise if $S$ has an equivalent local martingale measure but not an equivalent martingale measure. Arbitrage appears only if no equivalent local martingale measure exists.*

Then, to exclude arbitrage opportunities from the market, we define the process $L = \{L_t, t \in [0, T]\}$ by setting

$$L_t := \frac{dQ}{dP}\bigg|_{\mathcal{F}_t} = \exp\left(-\int_0^t \lambda_u dV_u - \frac{1}{2}\int_0^t \lambda_u^2 du - \int_0^t \gamma_u dZ_u - \frac{1}{2}\int_0^t \gamma_u^2 du\right), \qquad t \in [0, T], \tag{22}$$

where $\lambda = \{\lambda_t, \ t \in [0, T]\}$ and $\gamma = \{\gamma_t, \ t \in [0, T]\}$ are $\mathbb{F}$-adapted processes satisfying the integrability conditions $\int_0^T \lambda_u^2 du < \infty$ $P$-a.s. and $\int_0^T \gamma_u^2 du < \infty$ $P$-a.s., respectively. The (local) martingale property of the discounted Bitcoin price process $S$ under $Q$ implies the following condition:

$$\mu_S A_t = \sigma_S \sqrt{A_t}(\lambda_t \bar{\rho} + \gamma_t \rho), \qquad t \in [0, T], \qquad P - \text{a.s.}. \tag{23}$$

To ensure that $L$ provides the density process of a probability measure equivalent to $P$, we require that $E[L_T] = 1$, meaning that $L$ is an $(\mathbb{F}, P)$-martingale. The processes $\lambda$ and $\gamma$ are interpreted, respectively, as the risk premium and the risk perception associated to the future direction or future possible movements of the Bitcoin market. For each choice of the process $\gamma$, the process $\lambda$ is fixed by Eq. (23), that is,

$$\lambda_t = \frac{1}{\bar{\rho}}\left(\frac{\mu_S \sqrt{A_t}}{\sigma_S} - \rho \gamma_t\right), \qquad t \in [0, T], \tag{24}$$

and we can consider the corresponding family of equivalent (local) martingale measures $Q^\gamma$ for $S$ parameterized by the process $\gamma$. To check if there are stock bubbles in the underlying market model, we study under which conditions the discounted Bitcoin price is a strict $(\mathbb{F}, P)$-local martingale with respect to an equivalent local martingale measure $Q^\gamma$. By applying Girsanov's theorem, the dynamics of the model under $Q^\gamma$ is described by the following equations:

$$\begin{cases} dS_t = \sigma_S \sqrt{A_t} S_t \left(\rho d\tilde{Z}_t + \bar{\rho} d\tilde{V}_t\right), & S_0 = s_0 \in \mathbb{R}^+, \\ dA_t = \left(\mu_A - \sigma_A \gamma_t\right) A_t dt + \sigma_A A_t d\tilde{Z}_t, & A_0 = a_0 \in \mathbb{R}^+, \end{cases} \tag{25}$$

where the $\mathbb{R}^2$-valued process $(\tilde{V}, \tilde{Z}) = \left\{\left(\tilde{V}_t, \tilde{Z}_t\right), t \in [0, T]\right\}$ defined by $\tilde{V}_t := V_t + \int_0^t \lambda_u du,$.

$\tilde{Z}_t := Z_t + \int_0^t \gamma_u du,$ is an $(\mathbb{F}, Q^\gamma)$-standard Brownian motion.

Now, suppose that the risk perception process is zero, that is, $\gamma \equiv 0$. Then, the change of measure from $P$ to $Q^0$ is well-defined since the associated density process $M = \{M_t, t \in [0, T]\}$ satisfying

$$\begin{cases} dM_t = -\dfrac{\mu_S}{\bar{\rho}\sigma_S}\sqrt{A_t}M_t dV_t, & M_0 = 1, \\ dA_t = \mu_A A_t dt + \sigma_A A_t dZ_t, & A_0 = a_0. \end{cases} \tag{26}$$

is a true $(\mathbb{F}, P)$-martingale thanks to [27]. We have the following result, which allows to detect the presence of bubbles in this setting.

**Proposition 4.3.** *In the model outlined in Eq.* (24), *the Bitcoin price process S has a bubble on* $[0, T]$ *if and only if* $\rho > 0$.

The proof is based on the application of some of Sin's results given in [27], where the existence of risk-neutral measures for the Hull-White stochastic volatility model [19] and for similar frameworks is determined by the possibility of explosion in finite time for solutions of certain auxiliary stochastic differential equations. Precisely, it is possible to show that the martingale property of the discounted stock price $S$ under $Q^0$, given in Eq. (25) with $\gamma = 0$, is fulfilled if and only if $\rho \leq 0$. Hence, a bubble arises if and only if the correlation parameter between stock returns and market attention is positive.

## 6. Toward a multiexchange generalization

Let us generalize the model introduced in Eq. (1) by assuming a possible delay $\tau$ for the attention factor to affect the Bitcoin price dynamics. Assume that the attention factor has been observed or is described by a deterministic function for $t \in [-l, 0]$ with $l \geq \tau$. We get

$$\begin{cases} \dfrac{dS_t}{S_t} = \mu_S A_{t-\tau} dt + \sigma_S \sqrt{A_{t-\tau}} dW_t, \; S_0 = s_0 \in \mathbb{R}^+, \\ dA_t = \mu_p A_t dt + \sigma_A A_t dZ_t, \; A_t = \varphi(t) \text{ for } t \in [-l, 0], \end{cases} \tag{27}$$

where $\varphi : [-l, 0] \to \mathbb{R}^+$.

Analogous results as those in Section 2 can be derived by similar computations, and model parameters, for a fixed delay, can be estimated by means of the maximum likelihood method. In order to estimate the delay parameter, we maximize the profile likelihood as defined in [15]. Details of this procedure can be found in [10]. The estimation results of model in Eq. (27) on the same daily data considered in Section 2 are summed up in **Table 3**.

In **Figure 3**, we plot simulated trajectories of the price process in Eq. (27) by letting the delay parameter vary.

| | $\tau$ | $\widehat{\mu}_A$ | $\widehat{\sigma}_A$ | $\widehat{\mu}_S$ | $\widehat{\sigma}_S$ |
|---|---|---|---|---|---|
| $A = Vol$ | 1 day | 0.4881 | 1.0459 | 0.0282 | 0.0924 |
| $A = SVI$ | 7 days | 1.0964 | 0.9946 | 0.1005 | 0.1885 |

**Table 3.** Parameter estimates for model in Eq. (27) fitted on daily observations from January 2015 to June 2017.

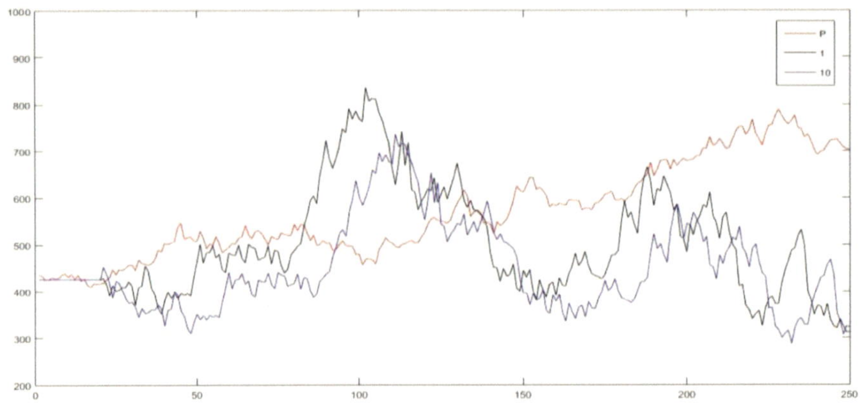


**Figure 3.** Simulated trajectories of $n = 250$ daily observations of the attention factor (red) and the Bitcoin price according to model in Eq. (27) when the delay parameter is $\tau = 1$ day (black) and $\tau = 10$ days (blue).

The different delays result in a shift to the south-east between the faster and slower reacting trajectories; in the picture, this behavior is sharp since the other model parameters are kept constant. By looking at the picture, the idea to model the price of Bitcoin in different exchanges by the same model in Eq. (27) but allowing different parameters naturally arises.

In particular, considering for instance two exchanges, we have

$$\begin{cases} \dfrac{dS_t^1}{S_t^1} = \mu_S^1 A_{t-\tau_1} dt + \sigma_S^1 \sqrt{A_{t-\tau_1}} dW_t, \quad S_0^1 = s_0^1 \in \mathbb{R}^+, \\ \dfrac{dS_t^2}{S_t^2} = \mu_S^2 A_{t-\tau_2} dt + \sigma_S^2 \sqrt{A_{t-\tau_2}} dW_t, \quad S_0^2 = s_0^2 \in \mathbb{R}^+, \\ dA_t = \mu_A A_t dt + \sigma_A A_t dZ_t, \quad A_t = \varphi(t) \text{ for } t \in [-l, 0], \end{cases} \tag{28}$$

where $\varphi : [-l, 0] \to \mathbb{R}^+$ with $l > \max\{\tau_1, \tau_2\}$ and $\mu_A^i, \mu_S^i, \sigma_A^i > 0, \sigma_S^i > 0$ for $i = 1, 2$ are constant parameters.

Note that within this model, prices for Bitcoin traded in different exchanges are perfectly correlated. Indeed, this is what happens in observed data; considering daily prices from January 2015 to June 2017 for Bitstamp, Kraken, Cex.io, Gdax, and The Rock exchanges we get cross-correlation values larger than 0.999.

We fit model in Eq. (28) for the Bitstamp and Gdax exchanges on daily observations of Bitcoin price from January 2015 to June 2017 obtaining the outcomes reported in **Table 4**, when the

| Exchange | $\tau$ | $\mu_A$ | $\sigma_A$ | $\mu_S$ | $\sigma_S$ |
|---|---|---|---|---|---|
| Bitstamp | 1 | 0.4994 | 1.0461 | 0.0281 | 0.0896 |
| Gdax | 2 | 0.4997 | 1.0420 | 0.0326 | 0.1036 |

**Table 4.** Model fitting with delay parameter: outcomes for Bitstamp and Gdax exchanges when attention is measured by the trading volume.

| Exchange | $\tau$ | $\mu_A$ | $\sigma_A$ | $\mu_S$ | $\sigma_S$ |
|---|---|---|---|---|---|
| Bitstamp | 7 days | 1.0934 | 0.9946 | 0.0992 | 0.1782 |
| Gdax | 7 days | 1.0964 | 0.9946 | 0.1160 | 0.2087 |

**Table 5.** Model fitting with delay parameter: outcomes for Bitstamp and Gdax exchanges when attention is measured by the SVI index.

attention is measured by the trading volume, and in **Table 5**, when attention is measured by the Google SVI index.

It is evident from the outcomes in **Table 4** that the model parameters are not significantly different while the delay might be quite different as if the reaction to the attention factor is faster for some exchanges and slower for others. On the contrary, when attention is measured by the Google SVI Index, the delay is unchanged, but the difference between estimated parameters for the price dynamics is nonnegligible.

By analyzing the outcomes and considering the shift effect as depicted in **Figure 3**, it is tempting to conjecture that the faster reaction determines the leader exchanges and that the slower exchange will then follow. If we could forecast that the next day price of the slower exchange will reach the price today for the faster one, we could obtain a profit by suitably investing in the two exchanges. However, it is worth noticing that the estimation of the delay parameter is obtained by maximizing the likelihood over a whole time series and is a product of averaging so arbitrage cannot be achieved in a direct way.

Nevertheless, in a multivariate setting as ours, the theory guarantees that arbitrage opportunities are ruled out if the market price of risk in the market is unique. Without entering technical details and assuming $r = 0$ for the sake of simplicity, this is true if and only if

$$\frac{\mu_S^1}{\sigma_S^1}\sqrt{A_{t-\tau_1}} = \frac{\mu_S^2}{\sigma_S^2}\sqrt{A_{t-\tau_2}}, \quad t \geq 0. \tag{29}$$

It is evident that these values are not equal if we plug parameter estimates in Eq. (30); hence, arbitrage opportunities are not ruled out at least from a theoretical point of view. We will address this issue more precisely in future research.

## 7. Conclusion

In this chapter, we have introduced a model in continuous time in order to describe the dynamics of Bitcoin price depending on an exogenous stochastic factor, which represents market attention on the Bitcoin system. Market attention is measured either by the total trading volume in Bitcoins or by means of the Google Search Volume Index, which, as suggested in [16], is a direct measure of the revealed attention for uniformed retail investors. More precisely, the attention factor affects directly the instantaneous mean and volatility of logarithmic returns; in addition, it may be also correlated with the price changes. An estimation procedure to fit the model to observed data is also suggested and, under the assumption of no correlation, a closed formula for standard European option prices on Bitcoin is provided.

By applying outcomes within the mathematical theory of bubbles [23–25, 27], we are able to show that Bitcoin boosts in a bubble if and only if there is a positive correlation between changes in the price and in the attention factor. This finding is reasonable and claims that a stronger positive dependence between the two processes in Eq. (21) may result in an explosion of the price process.

Finally, we allow for a delay on the effect of market attention on the Bitcoin price, and, based on this generalized model, we introduce a multivariate setting for our model (Eq. (28)) in order to take into account the special feature of multiple exchanges where it is possible to trade in Bitcoins. Preliminary results indicate that arbitrage opportunities may arise in two exchanges that are characterized by different delays.

## Acknowledgements

We gratefully acknowledge Marco Patacca for having provided the routines in Matlab® to develop the empirical sections of the paper and for useful suggestions and comments. We also acknowledge funding from Fondazione Cassa di Risparmio di Perugia (Grant 2015:0459013) and Bank of Italy (Grant 407660/16).

## Conflict of interest

The authors declare no conflict of interest.

## Thanks

Gianna Figà-Talamanca gratefully acknowledges interesting discussions on the topic of this chapter with colleagues of the Department of Finance and Risk Engineering where she was visiting professor while preparing this research. The authors also wish to thank Stefano Bistarelli for having introduced them to the intriguing and worth to explore world of cryptocurrencies.

## Author details

Alessandra Cretarola[1]* and Gianna Figà-Talamanca[2]

*Address all correspondence to: alessandra.cretarola@unipg.it

1 Department of Mathematics and Computer Science, University of Perugia, Perugia, Italy

2 Department of Economics, University of Perugia, Perugia, Italy

## References

[1] Nakamoto S. Bitcoin: A Peer-To-Peer Electronic Cash System. 2009. http://www.Bitcoin.org

[2] Urquhart A. The inefficiency of bitcoin. Economics Letters. 2016;**148**:80-82

[3] Dyhrberg AO. Bitcoin, gold and the dollar–A garch volatility analysis. Finance Research Letters. 2016;**16**:85-92

[4] Katsiampa P. Volatility estimation for bitcoin: A comparison of garch models. Economics Letters. 2017;**158**:3-6

[5] Kristoufek L. BitCoin meets Google trends and Wikipedia: Quantifying the relationship between phenomena of the internet era. Scientific Reports. 2013;**3**(3415):1-7

[6] Kristoufek L. What are the main drivers of the bitcoin price? Evidence from wavelet coherence analysis. PLoS One. 2015;**10**(4):e0123923

[7] Bukovina J, Marticek M. Sentiment and bitcoin volatility. Technical report, Mendel University in Brno, Faculty of Business and Economics; 2016

[8] Figà-Talamanca G, Patacca M. Does market attention affect Bitcoin returns and volatility? SSRN Electronic Journal. 2018:11

[9] Blau BM. Price dynamics and speculative trading in bitcoin. Research in International Business and Finance. 2017;**41**:493-499

[10] Cretarola A, Figà-Talamanca G, Patacca M. Market Attention and Bitcoin Price Modeling: Theory, Estimation and Option Pricing. Submitted; 2018

[11] Kim YB, Lee SH, Kang SJ, Choi MJ, Lee J, Kim CH. Virtual world currency value fluctuation prediction system based on user sentiment analysis. PLoS One. 2015;**10**(8):e0132944

[12] Yermack D. Is bitcoin a real currency? An economic appraisal. In: Handbook of Digital Currency. USA: Academic Press; 2015. pp. 31-43

[13] Levy E. Pricing European average rate currency options. Journal of International Money and Finance. 1992;**11**(5):474-491

[14] Davison AC. Statistical Models, Volume 11. USA: Cambridge University Press; 2003

[15] Pawitan Y. In all Likelihood: Statistical Modelling and Inference Using Likelihood. UK: Oxford University Press; 2001

[16] Da Z, Engelberg J, Gao P. In search of attention. The Journal of Finance. 2011;**66**(5):1461-1499

[17] Föllmer H, Schweizer M, Hedging of contingent claims under incomplete information. In M.H.A Davis and R.J.Elliot, editors, Applied Stochastic Analysis. New York, Gordon and Breach. 1991;**5**:389-414

[18] Föllmer H, Schweizer M. Minimal martingale measure. In: Encyclopedia of Quantitative Finance. Wiley Online Library; 2010

[19] Hull J, White A. The pricing of options on assets with stochastic volatilities. The Journal of Finance. 1987;**42**(2):281-300

[20] Black F, Scholes M. The pricing of options and corporate liabilities. The Journal of Political Economy. 1973:**81**(3):637-654

[21] Malhotra A, Maloo M. Bitcoin–Is it a bubble? Evidence from unit root tests. SSRN Electronic Journal. 2014:13

[22] Corbet S, Lucey B, Yarovya L. Datestamping the Bitcoin and Ethereum bubbles. Finance Research Letters. 2017:8 (In press)

[23] Jarrow RA, Protter PE, Shimbo K. Asset price bubbles in incomplete markets. Mathematical Finance. 2010;**20**(2):145-185

[24] Protter PE. A mathematical theory of financial bubbles. In: Paris-Princeton Lectures on Mathematical Finance. Switzerland: Springer; 2013. pp. 1-108

[25] Protter PE. Bubbles and crashes - mathematical models of bubbles. Quantitative Finance Letters. 2016;**4**:10-13

[26] Protter PE. Stochastic Integration and Differential Equations. Germany: Springer; 2005

[27] Sin CA. Complications with stochastic volatility models. Advances in Applied Probability. 1998;**30**(1):256-268

Section 2

# Blockchain and Digital Returns

Chapter 2

# Blockchain and Digital Currency in the World of Finance

Tatjana Boshkov

Additional information is available at the end of the chapter

http://dx.doi.org/10.5772/intechopen.79456

**Abstract**

High-tech enables payment evolution and global competition. The ambiguities surrounding of the digital currency still leave enough space for the analysis of its unreserved acceptance, trust and anticipation, which are the main driver for the spread of the network. Banks should carefully consider the technology underlying these cryptocurrencies as a potential generic new way of transferring ownership of the value over the long term. The chapter provides an analysis of the use of cryptocurrencies in general, especially Bitcoin as the technology adoption in the presence of network externalities. The objective attitude is the future of the digital currency in the moment is still unsolved issue due to the existence of "critical mass". Further, the chapter explores financial privacy which is very sensitive issue in using digital currency (or cryptocurrency) and discuss about private choices versus political rules. The research has shown that the future of cryptocurrencies can be bright if some institutional-formal conditions are met due to the fact that success evolution of e-money requires building safety payments through three criteria–standardization, compatibility and innovation.

**Keywords:** Blockchain, digital currency, network externalities, critical mass, technology, payment evolution

## 1. Introduction

Electronic money is not a new phenomenon. Trade over the Internet has increased the use of new technologies, thereby increasing the demand for new electronic payment methods. What really is new is electronic payment in retail and use of the Internet as new monetary market. Today, money becomes ready information on the microprocessor or in the database. Without a doubt, the purpose of such an instrument is to improve the efficiency of the traditional payment method. At this moment, there are still no clear standards in the Blockchain mechanism and therefore we do not know the boundaries, so participants can easily communicate without the presence of a regulator. Behind Blockchain technology is the universal Internet currency, which in turn raises many questions about the utilization of the advantages and risks/damages that would be arisen from the application.

High-tech enables payment evolution and global competition. But still the ambiguities surrounding the use of the digital currency leave enough space for the analysis of its unreserved acceptance, trust and anticipation, which are the main driver for the spread of the network. More precisely, the spread of the network requires interdependence of demand, which means the Network, must reach the minimum required volume before it reaches a balance. The minimum volume of the network is called "critical mass". Therefore, the objective attitude is the future of the digital currency in the moment is still unsolved issue due to the existence of "critical mass".

This chapter underlines the technology adoption in the presence of network externalities. Payment innovations that involve the creation of a network between the manufacturer and the consumer are product that inevitably involves network externalities that must touch the critical mass of the user before it starts to use it successfully. Network externalities exist due to the average consumer benefits from such an instrument, only if other consumers and traders use the same payment instrument.

Further, the chapter explores financial privacy which is very sensitive issue in using digital currency (or cryptocurrency). The analysis explores what are the private choices versus political rules. Success evolution of e-money requires building safety payments through three criteria—standardization, compatibility and innovation.

The diffusion that digital currency brings in the modern era expands the antitrust issues related to network externalities and global competition between most explored world currencies. This is the reason to include a review of social costs and benefits, as possible risks of using digital currency. These mean that in order to remain compatible with each other, all users should use software that meets the same rules. Therefore, all users and developers have a strong incentive to protect this consensus and set up a regulator.

At the end, the chapter examines the question—are there prospects of taking hand in hand the technology revolution and monetary evolution without risks in the real world?!

## 2. Overview of the IT revolution and innovations related to money

The online trade increased the use of new technologies, and thus increased the demand for new electronic payment methods. This began especially in the mid-1990s with the information revolution, the decline in computer prices and the networking of the same. Cohen introduces the term "change the geography of money" [1]. This term occurs as a result of the electronic payment in retail and use of the Internet as a new monetary market. Due to the information revolution, a new electronic payment method has been introduced, known as electronic cash, e-bag, e-currency, digital currency, digital money or digital cash. Without a doubt, the purpose of such an instrument is to improve the efficiency of the traditional payment method.

Bitcoin is a digital currency whose value varies according to the worldwide customer acceptance. This is primarily due to the fact that, unlike the standard currencies we use, such as the dollar or the euro, which are regulated by central banks, for Bitcoin there is no regulation. Therefore, transactions with Bitcoin are considered more private and anonymous due to the open system and no existence of a regulatory body and/or intermediary in the performance of transactions.

Transactions are carried out using cryptographic protection, and their execution is done through a network of public electronic books called "ledgers". For verification of transactions, it is necessary to have specific hardware and software that users can set up and after a certain number of transactions they receive a proportion of Bitcoin. In this way, it is also performed an additional commissioning of this digital currency.

### 2.1. Development of e-payment and digital currency

From the aspect of the development of e-payment method, digital currency is not physically printed by the Central Bank. For now, digital currency is considered with its own rules of the game. In the literature, all those who support the use of Bitcoin underscore the characteristic as a currency that does not cause financial crises. Namely, the view is that banks can print more money to cover their national debt, thus devaluing their currencies, Bitcoin does not function in such a way.

Electronic payment method exists from the 1960s, i.e. from the development of Electronic Funds Transfer (EFT), which became more sophisticated and applicable in a growing number of countries [2]. EFT implies the application of computer and telecommunication technology in payment. This method was used by banks and other financial institutions to exchange and transfer a large amount of money on a national and international level. The basis for the operation of EFT is that the money moves through a network as a substitute for cash or checks to execute a transaction. In this way, the time for paying should be shortened and the transaction costs reduced. The use of EFT has significantly increased with the emergence and acceptance of ATMs, which allow money transfer at the point of sale (EFTPOS). EFT is considered as first degree in the electronization of transactions.

In the early 1980s, thanks to the development of network technology, the costs of telecommunications and data processing were reduced, and electronic payments became more useful with the appearance of credit and debit cards, which for several years (after their appearance) became the most popular electronic small transaction tool. Also, the development of encryption has played a major role in successful card payments. This innovation is considered as a second degree in the electronization of transactions.

The growth and acceptance of card payments had negative consequences for the traditional way of payment. Many countries have made a move from the use of paper instruments, such as cash and checks, to the use of electronic instruments. For the first time in many countries, the number of checks payments has been reduced. Namely, checks as a very popular payment instrument loose the market role, thereby reducing their use [3].

### 2.2. e-Payment and transaction costs

In classical trade payments require at least one buyer and one seller, both having to have accounts in banks that are connected through clearing houses. Payments with traditional instruments such as checks require intervention of a financial intermediary like bank. Payment with e-money is similar to the traditional scheme—there are two parties—one or two banks. However, the whole process becomes more efficient and easier. The transaction does not require any code and cannot exceed the previously defined amount. If the amount that is on the chip is fully spent, the card can be automatically refilled at the merchant, without charging any fees, thanks to the special POS mechanism [4].

Once the chip is full, the user does not need to require an ATM or an exact amount of cash. Additionally, the problem of stealing or losing money is reduced to a minimum. An e-money transaction does not require an intermediary at present because the money expressed in units (called bits) is electronically transferred from the buyer to the seller. The amount of money that has been paid is prepared at the seller's terminal, i.e. his account is transferred to the financial institution from time to time.

Payment with e-money reduces transaction costs, and time is shortened compared to other forms of payment. Humphrey and colleagues estimate that the cost of using electronic money amounts to one third to half of the cost of paying paper money. When all transactions in one country would be carried out electronically, it would be possible to save more than 1% per year BDP.

### 2.3. A brief history of digital currency

From the era of barter economy, metal and coins to gold and silver, continuing to the modern monetary systems and checks, and ending with the latest developments in the global currency, such as the introduction of cryptocurrency like Bitcoin, have passed centuries. Each type of money plays a crucial role in transactional activities in some period of time. As human society and markets developed in particular, there was a need for more sophisticated instruments for the exchange of goods. In this regard, the introduction of cryptocurrency revolutionized the international payment system in a size that only a few years ago was unimaginable. The cryptocurrency is a digital or virtual currency that uses cryptography for security. Cryptocurrency is hard to forge because of this security feature. The determining characteristic of cryptocurrency, and probably the most attractive, is its organic nature as the fact that it is not issued by any central authority. Cryptocurrencies have their own advantages and disadvantages. The main benefits of using cryptocurrencies are that they transfer the funds more easily between two parties in the transaction [5]. These transactions are facilitated through the use of public and private keys for security purposes. These fund transfers are carried out with minimal processing costs, allowing users to avoid the large fees for online transactions charged by most banks.

There are two reasons for the emergence of electronic money and digital currencies. The first, according to the Austrian School of Economic Analysis money is a "social institution" subject to the already initiated institutional change and is interpreted as a consequence of a spontaneous evolution that should overcome the shortcomings of the swap and the double coincidence of desires [6, 7]. Today e-money is the last stage of this development and represents an additional degree of institutional change [8].

Their main role is to support online e-commerce, enable transactions, reduce their costs, or replace the payment of money and coins in retail. The second reason for the emergence of e-money is the information revolution, which is characterized by the integration of electronic information processing and telecommunication technologies, which reduces the geographical differences by means of which information can be transmitted to the whole world. The information revolution has changed the financial sector, making payment modes more secure and more efficient, giving an additional reason for the emergence of new monetary innovations [9].

Unlike the information revolution, the emergence of e-money is a new way of processing information for transferring purchasing power. Many financial innovations are not a new form of money, but a different way of using existing money in transactions [10]. Regardless of the consequences of the mentioned technological development, the nature of the money is still identical i.e. money serves as a means of exchange, as an asset and as a value. The nature of the money will never change, so the money will remain only an intermediary in the exchange of goods and services. e-Money card is a different payment method that allows electronic transfer of the value from the card to the terminal or from the card in the wallet, both in real time and through networks [11]. It is considered that e-money is the most important achievement that transfers the predetermined monetary value so it can be used for more transactions of lesser value. e-Pocket consists of a microcomputer that contains information about the monetary value that can be used. It is a higher degree of technological development compared to magnetic tape cards. Also, the e-pouch is more secure, which can reduce deception because cards with a chip can be more difficult to abuse than magnetic tape cards.

### 2.4. Reasons for Blockchain occurrence

Although cash is a quick and efficient payment method, the disadvantages of its use are numerous. Keeping cash is followed with many costs, including fraud, money loss, depositing, as well as the costs associated with managing money in financial institutions.

The purpose of e-money is replacing the cash in transactions of small values, thus avoiding its shortcomings, for example French experience with Moneo. Moneo is designed to reduce the cost of keeping cash and purchasing power to be temporarily transferred in a more efficient manner. This structure should be applied to various retail transactions of lesser value in order to eventually become a substitute for cash.

Moneo offers great advantages for consumers and retailers. Benefits for consumers are: greater transaction speed and potential benefit in the form of a discount on future purchases. Consumers do not have to have an exact amount of cash each time. There will be many mistakes in cash recovery. The owners of the Moneo card should carry fewer bank cards, especially if the features of debit and credit cards are included, and thus they would feel more secure [12]. Traders would receive cash before sending material goods or services, loyalty to customers would increase, the process of payment at the place of purchase would be speeded up, thereby reducing the processing costs of the transaction itself. If the benefit of using Moneo cards would be greater than the cost, retailers could pay to customers to use such a card [11].

If we make comparison between Moneo and POS, it turns out that the former has significant advantages over the POS. Namely, debit and credit cards are not as effective a payment method for low value transactions as transaction-related costs become higher for retailers and buyers, and e-money can be used with much lower costs. Paying for e-money is followed by much lower costs compared to other payment methods, primarily credit and debit cards. Another argument that accompanies the Moneo card is that it has a newer encryption technology compared to other cards, which increases security and limits the possibility of fraud. Because Moneo does not require any authorization or identification of the buyer, it allows additional reduction in transaction costs. The new technology of digital payments and currencies will allow real property to be used as a means of exchange.

How much e-money will be used depends largely on the motivation of its publishers, consumers and traders [13–15]. Consumers' demand will depend on the advantages and disadvantages of e-money in the form of payment, issuers' fees, consumer confidence in the use of e-money, ease of use, merchants' readiness to accept e-money. Motivation for the issuers covers the revenues from the collected fee from card users (traders and consumers), income from investing the remaining amount of money, i.e. for banks—issuers, savings of less retained cash, in the range in which e-money replaces cash). Potential shortcomings for publishers can be expected costs for future regulation. The willingness of retailers to accept e-money is closely related to the fee that will be charged by publishers or operators. For consumers and retailers the most important will be their willingness to embrace new technology. Most researchers believe that the use of e-money will be moderate in the short and medium term, while in the long run e-money can be very widespread.

## 3. The potential of cryptocurrency

There are different and confronted opinions regarding the future of cryptocurrencies in general. The optimistic view of the use of cryptocurrencies is supported by the fact that they easily transfer funds between two parties in the transaction. These transactions are facilitated by the use of public and private keys for security purposes. These fund transfers are made with minimal processing costs, allowing users to avoid large fees charged by most banks. In addition, many countries have begun to accept Bitcoin as a valid currency. In particular, countries that aim to get rid of cash have a very friendly approach to encryption. The argument that the promoters use for Bitcoin is the market capitalization of Bitcoin, ether and other cryptocurrencies, claiming that the cryptocurrency market has become very large and powerful, and the ban would be expensive for each country. Today, the total value of all cryptocurrencies has reached a record of value of more than $ 390 billion. This means that the market value of cryptocurrencies is greater than the value of the Citigroup. The new record was reached in December when the most famous cryptocurrency Bitcoin grew to $ 19,000.

Among other significant cryptocurrencies are Ripple and Ethereum. The cryptocurrency Ripple, designed for banks and global money transfers, has seen a major feat in the value of its digital currency that has risen in recent months. On December 10, the company had a market capitalization of just over $ 9 billion. In the end of December, its market value rose to a mere 51%, with a total value of $ 18.1 billion. Today it is worth $ 39 billion. Ripple's cryptocurrency is adopted by banks and other financial institutions. These companies believe that Ripple's system offers better prices and is more secure than other digital currencies, including Bitcoin. It allows users to send, receive and hold any currency in a decentralized way through the Ripple network. The company has a positive cash flow relationship and owns a huge shop on the XRP (Ripple Market), which is periodically released on the market. Investors who believe that cryptocurrencies can reach peak, are looking for others that could provide a greater return in the long run. However, the company has made some significant milestones in recent months. By the end of October 2017, Ripple licensed its Blockchain technologies to more than 100 banks. Its real attraction is the Ripple XRP system, which is ideal for banks because of its liquidity, speed and efficiency since the transaction lasts only 4 seconds, like no other cryptocurrency transaction.

However, the support for cryptocurrencies like Ripple is certainly superfluous and is something that should be understood by potential buyers and sellers because it gives those financial institutions a much higher level of control over Ripple than most other cryptocurrencies in the market. Bitcoin, Ethereum and other cryptocurrencies are completely decentralized, meaning that no one has real control over the network, Ripple's nodes are handled by Ripple Labs. These independent servers do not have to provide calculations for work evidence, such as Bitcoin, nodes simply validate transactions by themselves like traditional banks. Although the value of the Ethereum is not like Bitcoin, it is great for trading, and some of its more advanced features give exciting potential for the future.

Ethereum functions as well as most other cryptocurrencies. Ethereum token—Ether, works similar like Bitcoin. You can buy and sell with confirmation of transactions that are handled through the block. It is completely decentralized, without bank securing of the certificates needed to check the transactions. "Diggers" around the world fulfill this role by running powerful calculation algorithms. Completing these algorithms, the gob is rewarded with Ether, much like digging a Bitcoin that rewards with Bitcoin. As far as Ethereum and Bitcoin have some similarities, however, both platforms have different goals. Bitcoin is a strictly digital currency, designed to function as a means of payment or a warehouse with value, Ethereum takes a greater approach. Ethereum functions as a platform through which people can use ether tokens to create and execute applications and more importantly smart deals. Smart contracts are contracts written in the code, which the creator transfers to the block. Each time one of those contracts is executed, each node of the network executes it, set to Blockchain [16]. Thus, it is preserved in the public book, theoretically protected from evidence. Like other cryptocurrencies, Ethereum is prone to wild fluctuations in value. While Ethereum has risen high late, it is also susceptible to falls as well as other cryptocurrencies. Ethereum whether it is strong enough to survive a long run, or is a short-lived trend, remains on time.

From here we will conclude what are the advantages of the cryptocurrencies [17]:

- No inflation—the maximum number of coins is strictly limited (for example, 21 million in Bitcoin). Since there are neither political forces nor corporations that can change this order, there is no possibility of developing inflation in the system.
- Peer-to-peer cryptocurrency network—in such networks there is no master server, which is responsible for all operations. The exchange of information (in this case—money) is between 2 and 3 or more software customers. All installed by programmers-users who are part of the network. Each client stores a record of all transactions executed and the number in each wallet. Transactions are made from hundreds of distributed servers. Neither banks nor taxes, nor governments can control the exchange of money between.

- Unlimited possibilities for a transaction—each of the wallet holders can pay to everyone, anywhere and any amount. The transaction cannot be controlled or prevented, so you can make transfers anywhere in the world wherever a user is placed with a wallet.
- No borders—payments made in this system are impossible for cancelation. Coins cannot be forged, copied or spent twice. These opportunities guarantee the integrity of the field system.
- Decentralization—there is no central controlling authority in the network, the network is alluded to all participants, each computer crypto-valued member is a member of this system. This means that the central government has no power to dictate rules to cryptocurrency owners. And even if some part of the network goes offline, the payment system will continue to function steadily.
- Anonymity—completely anonymously and at the same time completely transparent. Each company can create an infinite number of crypto address addresses, regardless of name, address, or any other information.
- Transparency—Bitcoin stores the history of transactions that have ever happened. It is called a sequential block of blocks or a blockhead. The block keeps information about everything. So, if the company publicly uses the Bitcoin address for example, then everyone can see how much Bitcoin is owned. If the address of the company is not publicly confirmed, then nobody will ever know that it belongs to this company. For full anonymity, companies use the unique bitcoin address for each transaction.
- Bitcoin's open digging code applies the same algorithms used in online banking. The only difference in online banking is the disclosure of information to users. All information about the transaction in the BTC network is shared (like, when), but there is no data for the recipient or the sender of the currencies (no access to the owner's personal data).
- Transaction speed—the ability to send money everywhere and everyone within minutes after the network of the crypto-currency will process the payment.

## 4. The omission and risks of cryptocurrencies

Cryptocurrency opponents argue that cryptocurrencies are highly unstable, can be used for money laundering or financing illegal activities. In this regard, Humphrey, for example, is giving reasons why the cryptocurrency is not a viable electronic currency [18] . He notes that Bitcoin is illiquid and has shown price volatility and that the discounted monetary value of Bitcoin is zero. Further, he notes that the currency does not have a central issuer, and that there is no financial or economic basis for its creation. They are:

- Strong instability—almost all the ups and downs of the value of some cryptocurrencies. This instability creates the problem in the short term.
- Difficult to understand—crypto-valves are relatively new and come with a learning curve. People end up investing without proper knowledge and are losing money for something they have not learned.

- Lack of knowledge—people are not aware of how to use cyberattacks and hence be exposed to hackers. The technology is somewhat complex and therefore we need to educate ourselves before investing.
- There is no way to cancel the payment—if you're mistaken for someone using the cryptocurrency, then there is no way to get a refund of the amount paid. All you can do is asking the person to return the funds and if your request is denied, then just forget the money.
- Major risks for investing in cryptocurrencies that need to be considered in the medium and long term.

Many experts believe that the list of deficiencies in crypto-voltages is much longer and related to the risk of money laundering, terrorist financing and other illegal activities, the lack of a central publisher, which means that there is no legal formal guarantee person in the case of bankruptcy, and the like. Although it is very difficult to predict, many academics and professionals in this topic argue that the future of cryptocurrency is bright because it will remove trade barriers and intermediaries, reduce transaction costs, thereby boosting trade and the economy.

## 5. Anticipation of Bitcoin acceptance and "critical mass"

Analyzing the process of money accepting, shows that money is usable as individuals believe that others will be used them for different needs in society. Krueger believes that individuals will accept the e-money system as long as its value is compounded and not reduced drastically [19]. The fact that the individual accepts the money stems from what others accept. Anticipating factor is the key determinant of accepting money. Acceptance, trust and anticipation are the basic factors that enable the spread of the network. However, these factors are not enough because the size of the network also requires interdependence of demand, which means that the network must reach the minimum required size before it reaches a balance. Economides and Himmelberg such a minimal magnitude of the network determinate as "critical mass" [20]. Oliver defined the critical mass as "a smaller segment of the population that wants to make a big contribution to collective action, while most work little or nothing" [21]. A critical mass or starting base plays a key role in the development of the network.

Electronic money cards, like other innovations that involve creation of a network between the manufacturer and the consumer, are a product that inevitably involves the network externality must touch the critical mass of the user before starting to use it successfully. The indicated phenomenon in literature is called a two-sided market. The development of the payment instrument first depends on two types of externalities associated with their application and use. The outsourcing of the network exists because the average consumer benefits from such an instrument, only if other consumers and traders use the same payment instrument. Additionally, the total benefit from the use of e-money card exceeds the usage limit realized by the individual consumer. By accessing one user to the network, the benefits for other users are increased.

Thus, the user's critical mass will be achieved when the demand-side dependency between retailers and consumers will not be more economically significant, i.e. when the expectations of the consumer benefit will not significantly change depending on the new members of the network [22]. Consumer benefits will increase when more merchants accept the new payment instrument, while the commercial benefit will increase if consumers use the new instrument more often. Additionally, the attractiveness of such an instrument can be reduced due to the incompatibility and competitiveness of the composition, as in the case of video recorders a few decades ago [23].

The use and distribution of the network is a complex issue because the interdependence of demand will remain an obstacle until the network reaches a critical mass, either independently or with the help of a regulator. According to the analyses of Katza and Shapira the growth of the network in its nature can be self-fulfilling [24]. Accomplish a critical mass in using Blockchain is not easy because traders must invest in special POS devices to be able to use e-money; and consumers will have to use e-money in a retail transaction as a substitute for coins and paper money. The goal of this problem is to convince a large number of users to start using e-money.

One of the reasons that few people use this payment method is precisely the habit of using cash for a retail transaction. At the same time, the banks' habits in carrying out a transaction may be the reason for the slow implementation of new insurances. Consumers gained confidence in financial intermediaries over time, and therefore did not get used to doing a transaction without their presence. Therefore, consumers are not ready for change. More consumers need more time to get to know the functioning of the new payment system. Accordingly, most of them would look forward to seeing the development of the situation because they want to gain more confidence before accepting innovation. As each phenomenon goes through stages of development, it is possible to expect further progress and an economy without cash using the digital economy.

## 6. Technology adoption in the presence of "network externalities"

The use of e-money is a complicated phenomenon and firstly depends on the interactions between users of products and services.

According to Schmalensee the network can be defined as a composition of directly or indirectly coupled nodes [25]. Schmalensee considered that the main hallmark of the network is the fact that there is a network externality. The above concept is often applied in economic literature; also often appears in the literature on industrial organizations and public finances [20, 26].

From a user's perspective, Bitcoin is a mobile application or a computer program that provides personal money, Bitcoin, and allows users to send and receive Bitcoins through them. This is the way how Bitcoin works for the most users. The network of Bitcoin is sharing a public book called "block chain". This book contains any transaction ever processed, allowing the user's computer to verify the validity of each transaction. The authenticity of each transaction is protected by digital signatures and corresponds to the sent address, allowing for all users to have complete control over the sent Bitcoins from their own Bitcoin addresses. So, anyone can perform processing of transactions using computer with specialized hardware, and earn Bitcoins for this service.

The term "network externalities" refers to the product or service to get better value for consumers, as many people use them and thus continuously increases the number of network users (a significant proportion of the value of the products or network refers to its other participants). This concept has positive spiral. It is often mentioned in relation to products used in digital technology, i.e. with products whose use significantly increases with the increase in the number of consumers.

Farrell et al., for the first time presented the Economic Analysis of the Network Outsourcing [24, 27]. They classified the network externalities into two groups-direct and indirect. Direct network externalities exist when increasing the size of the network increases the number of other users with whom it can be completely "communicated". In such a network there are inactions and complementarity between users of the same product or service. Indirect network externalities exist when increasing the size of the network increases the supply of products or services available for network users.

Network externality introduces dynamic elements for network users when deciding on entering the network, as well as for manufacturers of such products when making a production decision [16]. Consumers in the decision to enter the network must take into account the size of the network for the future. The companies are motivated to invest in building a network from which they would make a lease later.

## 7. Financial privacy: could Bitcoin hide the criminals?

Five years ago Bitcoin showed the opportunity for being anonymous. But this is changing starting with Federal Bureau of Investigation (FBI) and other law enforcement, for example. The biggest part of Bitcoin users are law-abiding people motivated by privacy concerns. Also there are people that see the anonymity as a tool for financial crime. This was a reason to show attempt for virtual currency regulation. It's well known that Governments are grappling with the virtual currencies as it continues to gain popularity. So, in 2013 the U.S. Department of Treasury issued Guide how to use digital currency and money transmitters. In that time was taken some steps for Bitcoin regulation, meaning that cryptocurrency should be threaten as a taxable property. Conducting transactions in digital currencies has emerged as one of the preferred payment methods because it provides anonymity and privacy. At the begging as it previous mention in the text, digital currency was subject of interest for criminals.

Bitcoins are transferred between transacting parties without an intermediary, thus offering providing level of privacy and anonymity. A public ledger contains the transactions as cryptographic representations, but no personal information is recorded. Exchanging Bitcoins in a transaction is much like exchanging cash, but through the Internet. In attempting to regulate digital currencies is that doing so dismantles a technology that fosters privacy. Regulation erodes the privacy linked with digital currency. Think of it as transacting in an account that is protected by strong secrecy laws. In order to regulate those transactions, the system has to eliminate the secrecy. Regulation of digital currencies would undermine the system as an enabler of privacy and reduce its appeal. Users who seek the opportunity of privacy in digital currencies will look to other venues to conduct their business, in countries with less regulation. But the consequence of regulation of digital currency will be enabling privacy violations because in such a circumstances business and individuals have to share information with the government and others [28]. These potential risks of having no regulation for digital currency distract many users in the world because there is no confidence [29].

A regulatory framework for digital currencies is more than need for public protection and combating criminal activities. However, caution should be exercised to avoid stifling the development of an innovative technology. Regulation of digital currencies should be sufficiently balanced with privacy, business development and innovative technology.

## 8. The way forward: technology revolution and monetary evolution

### 8.1. Key success factors

The current cryptocurrency market is highly competitive and fragmented. Experts identified more factors that will determine and rise the attractiveness and confidence in using cryptocurrency [30]:

The cryptocurrencies should be:

- Cost effective to issue
- Available immediately
- Governed and regulated
- Instantly liquid—liquidity should be instantly generated or generated
- on demand
- Secure and immutable—cannot be double spent
- Trusted—backed by a lender of last resort (e.g. a central bank)
- Free from fractional reserve banking in its crypto-form
- Transparent with transaction finality (directly or remotely)
- Add purpose to economic activity (commerce) and have sustainable value
- Have standards to enable interoperability
- Be legitimate—a competent authority to impose these standards

Cryptocurrencies will undoubtedly benefit market participants.

The benefits include [10, 29]:

- Immediate asset availability—the cryptocurrency will be available immediately for consumers and businesses to spend, without any waiting period.
- Immediate access to liquidity—the cryptocurrency will be highly liquid—liquidity generated instantly on demand.

- Free up working capital—the need for banks to hold reserves will be minimized as the money held for use as reserves will be available for other purposes thus optimizing intra-day liquidity.
- Transaction efficiency—cryptocurrency transactions are fast and immediate—they improve efficiency by cutting out the middle man and avoiding lengthy back-office reconciliation processes.
- Transaction security—central bank-issued cryptocurrency transactions can be tracked protecting security. Security is also enhanced as there is no double spending.
- Over and above these benefits, a central bank-issued cryptocurrency can have a much larger impact on the wider economy and for all market participants because it can:
- Boost economic growth—a central bank issued cryptocurrency can permanently boost economic growth.
- Act as an enabler for mobile and digital commerce—it can replace current immediate payment models by delivering the currency into the market in a more immediate, efficient and effective manner.
- Ensure stability in the financial system—a cryptocurrency can help maintain financial stability and provide policy makers with more effective tools to smooth out financial booms and busts. In periods of high inflation for fiat currencies, banks can hold cryptocurrencies, thus protecting their wealth.
- Work as a crypto-reserve currency—commercial banks can keep a portion of their reserves in cryptocurrency rather than in fiat currency, thus complementing the fractional reserve banking system.
- Effectively monitor the supply of money—a central bank issued cryptocurrency can help policy makers control the amount of money in the economy, as well as the supply of the cryptocurrency. This is currently not possible as banks create money by using deposits as loans.
- Lower costs—cryptocurrencies will enable the banking system to cut the costs of banknote issuance, circulation and handling. In addition, transaction costs will be significantly reduced especially for cross border transactions.
- Allow for traceability—transactions in central bank issued cryptocurrencies can be tracked, and simultaneously ensure that the users information remains protected, thus protecting privacy. A central bank issued currency follows KYB and KYC procedures which will allow the central bank to identify users when there is a need to.

Taking in an account that in the world of digital currency is needed regulation, increasing the attractiveness of using cryptocurrencies is found in support by central bank. The central bank with its authority and confidence that it has from the market participants, needs to do some reforms in the moment of deploying a cryptocurrency [31].

At the beginning, central bank is the most relevant factor to define the framework and standards for all participants. Regarding this, central bank can create and give policy guidance where all players will know policy and regulation very clear. Central bank following KYB and KYC procedures ensures control of financial criminal. In the moment when central bank issued cryptocurrency under legal framework it will have the status of legal tender.

The role of central banks raises more for all users in the economy. In the traditional way, central bank has no direct connection with consumers, which is a big difference when central bank issued cryptocurrency and has direct link with market participants.

## 9. Conclusion

The chapter was intended to provide an analysis for the use of cryptocurrencies in general and especially Bitcoin. The research has shown that the future of cryptocurrencies can be bright if some institutional-formal conditions are met. The advantages of using cryptocurrencies in trade facilitation, cost reduction and others are recognized by the majority of academics. Bitcoin and other cryptocurrencies have the potential to replace traditional and new payment methods. But in order to achieve this and become the dominant force in the global payment system, they must provide a distinctive individual value, deal with and overcome a number of critical challenges, such as formal regulatory issues. It is unlikely to happen in a short period of time. Also, banks should carefully consider the technology underlying these cryptocurrencies as a potential generic new way of transferring ownership of the value over the long term. On the other hand, we have seen that cryptocurrencies as a new rise in society constitute a new way of transparent and fluid flow of resources that can spur every economy.

The advances in information and communication technology enabled the development of new forms of electronic payment, both in the real world with card products and in the virtual world (software products). The reason for the growing prevalence of these products is precisely their great perceptions compared to the traditional way of payment. However, statistics confirm that the evolution of e-money is in the initial phase, and that cash is still the most important form of payment for retail transactions. Cash has not yet been replaced by any form of electronic payment. One of the reasons is precisely the fact that e-money is a rather sophisticated form of payment that requires some investment in new technology among retailers, as well as developing new experiences among the users. Therefore, the use of electronic money does not extend significantly.

Because Bitcoin is controlled by all users, and they are free to choose the software of their choice. Therefore, in order to maintain compatibility, users must change this, that is, they should use software that meets the same rules. Only Bitcoin can work properly with a complete consensus among all users. Ripple enabled us to look at how banks began to use it, in order to become more polyclinic in their work. The Ethereum has enabled us to get to know the extra possibilities of cryptocurrencies through Smart Arrangements. They could relieve individuals of the limitations of the legal system and big business.

Taking in account the success of cryptocurrencies, there is opinion that consumers, consortiums or large financial institutions would not be successful in launching cryptocurrencies. Further, here is believed that its success will be greater if the digital currencies are lunched by central banks. So, we should be thinking in using this tool more efficiency for the world economy, supportive than understanding them as possibility to disrupting the financial system. More detail, central bank has the authority to bring participants together and will increase the attractiveness of fiat money for exchange in clearing, payments and settlement. In this moment some experts asked two question according cryptocurrency and central banks. The first is linked with the deepness and preciseness of policy and economic implications of launching a central bank-issued cryptocurrency. The second issue is focused on impact of central bank-issued cryptocurrency on the banking system.

## Author details

Tatjana Boshkov

Address all correspondence to: tatjana.boshkov@gmail.com

Goce Delcev University, Shtip, Macedonia

## References

[1] Cohen BJ. The Future of Money, Chapter Seven. Princeton: Princeton University Press; 2004

[2] Bounie D, Abel F. Les déterminants de la détention et de l'usage des instruments de paiement: éléments théoriques et empiriques. Revue d'Economie Financière. 2006;**83**:159-173

[3] European Central Bank. The Blue Book. Bucharest: European Central Bank; 2005

[4] Baddeley M. Using E-cash in the new economy: An economic analysis of micropayment systems [online]. Journal of Electronic Commerce. 2004;**5**(4):239-253

[5] David P. Positive feedbacks and research productivity in science: Reopening another black box. In: Grandstrand O, editor. Economics of Technology. London: Elsevier Science; 1994. pp. 65-89

[6] Menger C. On the origin of money. Economic Journal. 1892;**2**(83):239-255

[7] von Hayek F. Denationalisation of Money: An Analysis of the Theory and Practice of Concurrent Currencies. Londres: Institute of Economic Affairs; 1976

[8] Schmitz SW. The institutional character of electronic money schemes: Redeemability and the unit of account. In: Latzer M, Schmitz SW, editors. Carl Menger and the Evolution of Payment Systems: From Barter to Electronic Money. Cheltenham, UK and Northampton, MA: Edward Elgar; 2001

[9] Goodhart CAE, Krueger M. The impact of technology on cash usage. The Magazine of De La Rue. 2001;(4):9-11

[10] White LH. The technology revolution and monetary evolution. In: Dorn JA, editor. The Future of Money in the Information Age. Washington, D.C.: CATO Institute; 1996

[11] Chakravorti S, Victor L. Payment instrument choice: The case of prepaid cards. Economic Perspectives. 2006;**2Q**:29-44

[12] Gerald S. The Electronic Purse: An Overview of Recent Development and Policy Issues. Bank of Canada; 1996

[13] BIS. Implications for Central Banks of the Development of Digital Money. Basel: Bank of International Settlements; 1996

[14] BIS. Survey of Developments in Electronic Money and Internet and Mobile Payments. Basel: Bank of International Settlements; 2004

[15] BIS. Statistics on Payment and Settlement Systems in Selected Countries. Basel: Bank of International Settlements; 2006

[16] Klenow JP. Evidence on Learning and Network Externalities in the Diffusion of Home Computers. Federal Reserve Bank of Minneapolis and NBER; 2002

[17] Centi JP. Currency competition and the monetary union. Unpublished PhD dissertation. Aix-Marseille University; 1979

[18] Humphrey D, Kim M, Vale B. Realizing the gains from electronic payments: Costs, pricing and payment choice. Journal of Money, Credit and Banking. 2001;**33**(2):216-234

[19] Krueger M. Toward a moneyless world. In: Paper Prepared for the International Atlantic Economic Conference Vienna; March 16-23, 1999

[20] Economides N, Himmelberg C. Critical mass and network evolution in telecommunications. In: Brock G, editor. Toward a Competitive Telecommunication Industry: Selected Papers for the 1994 Telecommunications Policy Research Conference. Mahwah, NJ: Lawrence Erlbaum; 1995. pp. 47-63

[21] Oliver PE, Marwell G, Teixeira R. A theory of the critical mass. I. Interdependence group heterogeneity, and the production of collective action. American Journal of Sociology. 1985;**91**:522-556

[22] Osterberg W, Thomson J. Network externalities: The Catch-22 of retail payment innovations. In: Economic Commentary. Federal Reserve Bank of Cleveland; 1998

[23] Stavins J. Effect of consumer characteristics on the use of payment instruments. Federal Reserve Bank of Boston New England Economic Review. 2001:20-31

[24] Katz ML, Shapiro C. Technology adoption in the presence of network externalities. Journal of Political Economy. 1986;**94**:822-841

[25] Schmalensee R. On antitrust issues related to networks. In: Testimony Before the Federal Trade Commission, Hearings on Global Competition/High-Tech Innovation, December 1. 1995

[26] Economides N. Economics of networks. International Journal of Industrial Organization. 1996;**14**:673-700

[27] Farrell J, Saloner G. Standardization, compatibility and innovation. RAND Journal of Economics. 1985;**16**:70-83

[28] Iwai K. 1997. Evolution of money. In: Paper Presented at the Workshop on Evolution and Economics; Certosa di Pontignano, Siena

[29] Stavins J. A comparison of social costs and benefits of paper check presentment and ECP with truncation. New England Economic Review (July/August). 1997;**12**:27-44

[30] Rahn RW. The future of financial privacy: Private choices versus political rules. In: The Future of Money and Financial Privacy, Chapter 6. 2000

[31] Mokyr J. Are we living in the middle of an industrial revolution? Federal Reserve Bank of Kansas City Economic Review. 1999;(14):31

Chapter 3

# Cryptocurrency Returns

Mike Cudd, Kristen Ritterbush,
Marcelo Eduardo and Chris Smith

Additional information is available at the end of the chapter

http://dx.doi.org/10.5772/intechopen.80397

**Abstract**

One of the most significant innovations in the world of finance has been the creation and evolvement of cryptocurrencies. These digital means of exchange have been the focus of extensive news coverage, especially the Bitcoin, with a primary focus on the tremendous potential return and the high level of accompanying risk. In this chapter, we examine the risk-return pattern for an array of cryptocurrencies, contrasting the pattern with those of conventional currency and equity investments. We find the measures of cryptocurrency returns and risk to be a very high multiple of those of conventional investments, and the pattern is determined to be robust relative to the time frame. Consequently, cryptocurrencies are determined to provide an alternative to investors that involves tremendously high risk and return.

**Keywords:** cryptocurrency, bitcoin, returns, risk

## 1. Introduction

This chapter is comprised of three sections. First, the risk-return characteristics of a broad array of cryptocurrencies are examined for a short holding period (i.e., the past year). Many of the cryptocurrencies are relatively new and were introduced at some point during the year 2017. Consequently, initially restricting the examination of cryptocurrency performance to the 2017 calendar year permits the inclusion of many of the new cryptocurrencies, which also provides a risk-return profile that is relevant to short-term investors. In addition, this provides an initial comparison of how these performance characteristics vary across the various cryptocurrencies. Second, the short-term performance of the largest four cryptocurrencies is contrasted with the performance of the largest four conventional currencies, and with the SP500 equity index. This provides a more focused performance profile of cryptocurrencies versus more conventional investments. Lastly, the risk-return profile is extended to the past 3 years to obtain a sense of the long-term pattern of performance. In this case, the examination is restricted to the only two cryptocurrencies that were publicly traded over this period; the Bitcoin and the Litecoin.[1] Again, the performance of the cryptocurrencies is contrast against the performance of the four major conventional currencies and the SP500 to provide a glimpse into the sustainability of the cryptocurrency risk-return patterns through longer periods of performance observation.

## 2. The cryptocurrency phenomenon and unconventional sources of risk

Through the cryptocurrency phenomenon, investors have been introduced to a whole new vocabulary consisting of terms such as block-chain, hash, nonce, proof-of-work, nodes, and other terms that apply to the cryptocurrency market structure [1]. The financial press addresses such topics as the irreversible design of cryptocurrency transactions (consensus protocol), the role of distributed cryptographic proof replacing the need for trust (i.e., the distributed ledger and transaction verification), privacy (i.e., anonymity), and the potential haven for transfers of illegally obtained funds, among others. Moreover, historically high returns offered by cryptocurrency investments over their limited lives have attracted the interest of speculating investors, as well as casual observers. The potential returns are enormous relative to those of more conventional investments, such as foreign currencies and the stock market, and the risks are commensurately higher.

Unconventional sources of risk also exist for the cryptocurrency market. Some researchers question the underlying foundation and source of value of cryptocurrencies [2–4]. The cryptocurrency market is also being pressured for adequate disclosure by the City of New York, targeted by the SEC, and more recently accused of market manipulation.[2] Even daytime talk shows have impacted the cryptocurrency market with negative comments by the world's most influential investor, Warren Buffett.[3]

Some studies suggest that the addition of cryptocurrencies to conventional investment portfolios may offer some diversification benefits [5], while other studies find limited diversification benefits to short-term investors [6], and some researchers question whether adding the Bitcoin to a conventional portfolio adds value [7]. Cryptocurrency investments are also observed to follow an asymmetric return pattern with fat distribution tails [8]. Furthermore, the largest cryptocurrency, the Bitcoin, is observed to be the most efficient of the cryptocurrencies [9].

Before proceeding to the examination of cryptocurrency performance, some of the more common names for the currency tickers are provided as a guide in navigating the graphics presented in this chapter (see **Table 1**).

---

[1] One study finds the Bitcoin and Litecoin to be the safest of the various cryptocurrencies [10].

[2] See [11–13].

[3] See [14].

http://dx.doi.org/10.5772/intechopen.80397

## 3. Short-term cryptocurrency performance comparison

Many of the cryptocurrencies only began publicly trading in the latter half of 2017 (refer to the inset in **Table 1** providing the month of initial trading).[4] Only the Bitcoin and Litecoin were in

| | |
|---|---|
| **Cryptocurrency** | |
| BTC | Bitcoin |
| ETH | Ethereum |
| XRP | Ripple |
| BCH | Bitcoin Cash |
| LTC | Litecoin |
| ADA | Cardano |
| XLM | Stellar |
| NEO | NEO |
| EOS | EOS |
| VEN | Vechain |
| IOT | IOTA |
| DASH | Digital Cash |
| TRX | Tronix |
| XEM | NEM |
| XMR | Monero |
| LSK | Lisk |
| ETC | Ethereum Classic |
| QTUM | QTUM |
| OMG | OmiseGo |
| **Conventional currency** | |
| GBP | British Pound |
| EUR | Euro |
| CHF | Swiss Franc |
| CAD | Canadian Dollar |
| **Stocks** | |
| SP500 | SP500 Stock Index |

**Table 1.** Currency names.

[4]For example, the Ethereum cryptocurrency was introduced in late 2013, funded by an online crowdsale in 2014. However, the system did not go live until July 2015 [15].

existence and publicly trading prior to 2015.[5] For this reason, cryptocurrency risks and returns are examined for different time segments.[6]

We begin by reviewing cryptocurrency returns for the year of 2017 in table form (see **Chart 1**). The horizontal bar chart provides both an analog and digital view of the enormous monthly returns and risks associated with the various cryptocurrencies. For example, the Tronix cryptocurrency (TRX) provided a 1049% monthly return over its roughly 4 months of trading ending the year

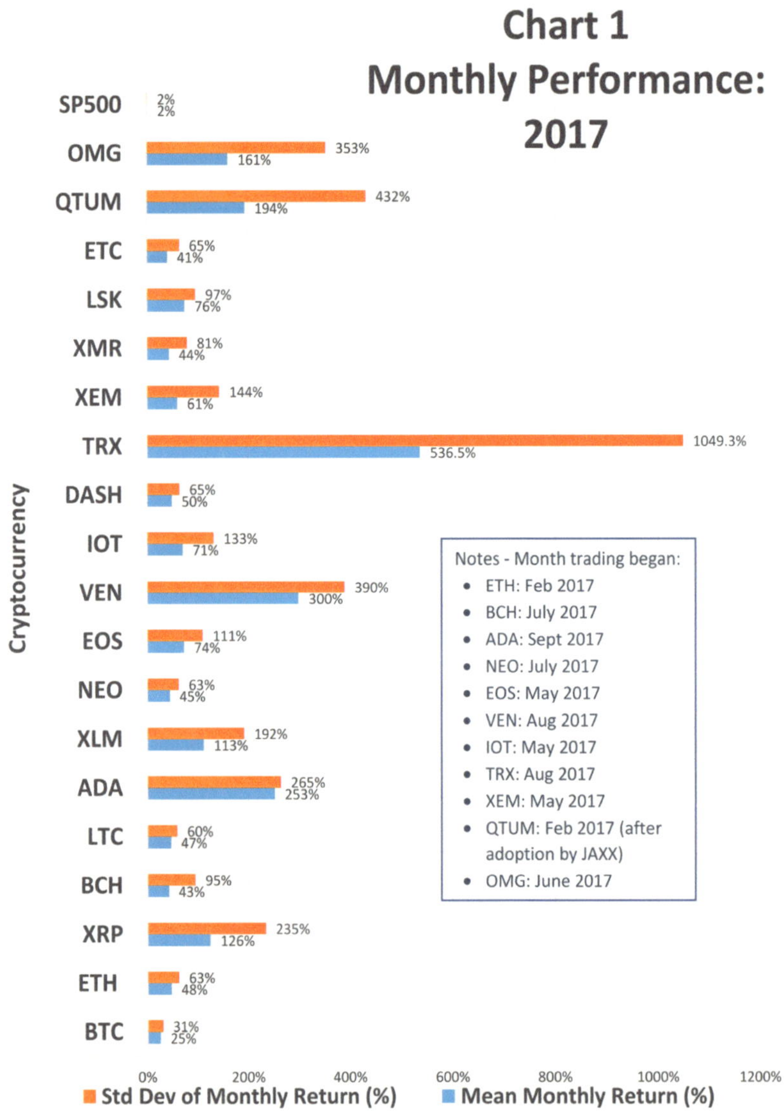


**Chart 1.** Cryptocurrency Risk-Return Performance: 2017.

---

[5] Source [16].

[6] All cryptocurrency, conventional currency, and SP500 returns are determined from adjusted prices obtained through [17].

2017 (i.e., it increased eightfold in value over the 4-month period). The SP500 risk-return performance is also included as a source of contrast. Note how each of the cryptocurrency measures of return and risk massively exceed those the SP500 index for the year 2017.

| | British Pound (%) | SP500 (%) | Bitcoin (%) |
|---|---|---|---|
| Monthly return | 0.8 | 1.8 | 30.8 |
| Standard deviation of return | 1.8 | 1.6 | 25.4 |

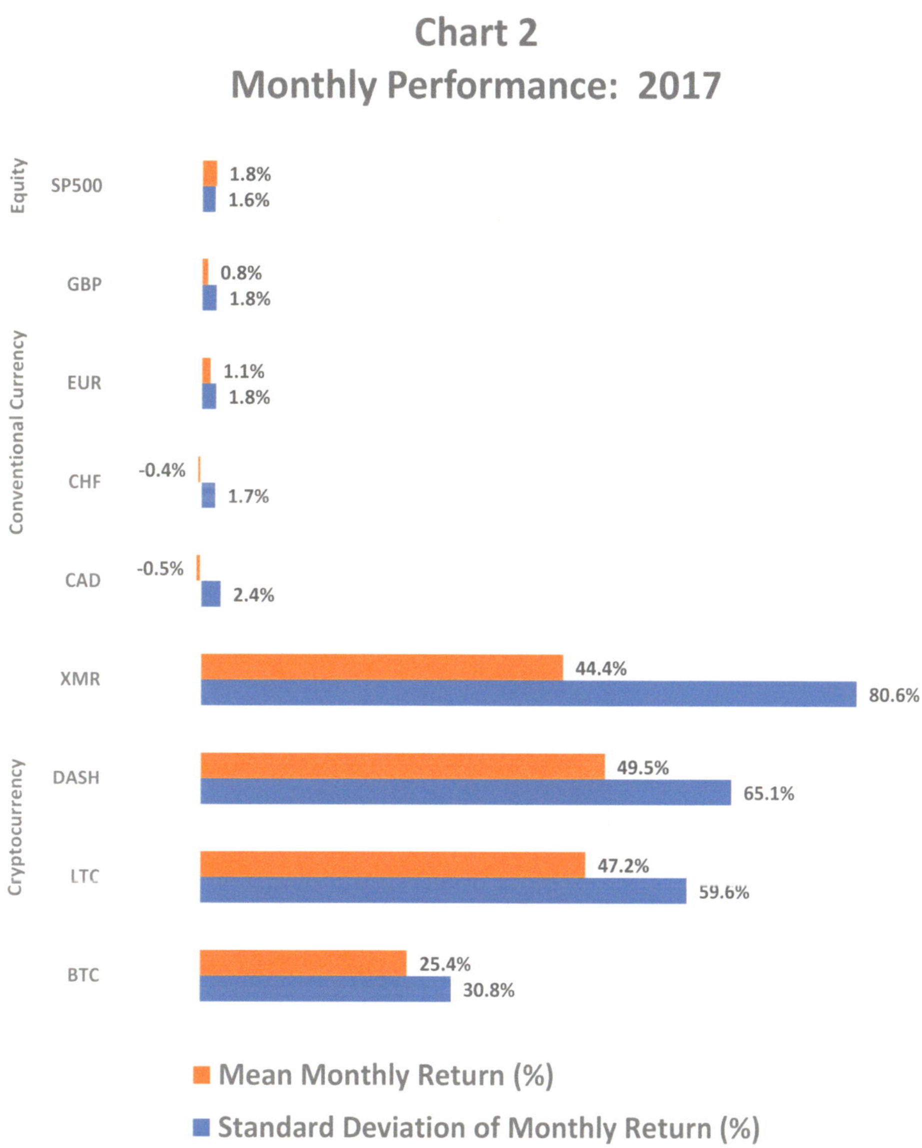


**Graph 1.** Major Cryptocurrency Risk-Return Pattern: 2017.

A different visual of the risk-return tradeoff across the various cryptocurrencies and the SP500 is presented in the form of a line graph (see **Graph 1**). As expected, there is a positive relationship between risk and return, with cryptocurrencies displaying higher monthly returns also carrying higher standard deviations of monthly return (i.e., higher risk). This graphic also depicts how the cryptocurrencies dominate the SP500 in terms of massively higher return and risk values.

Another contrast and sense of scale is obtained by comparing returns across different investment classes. For this purpose, we restrict our review to the four largest cryptocurrencies, the four

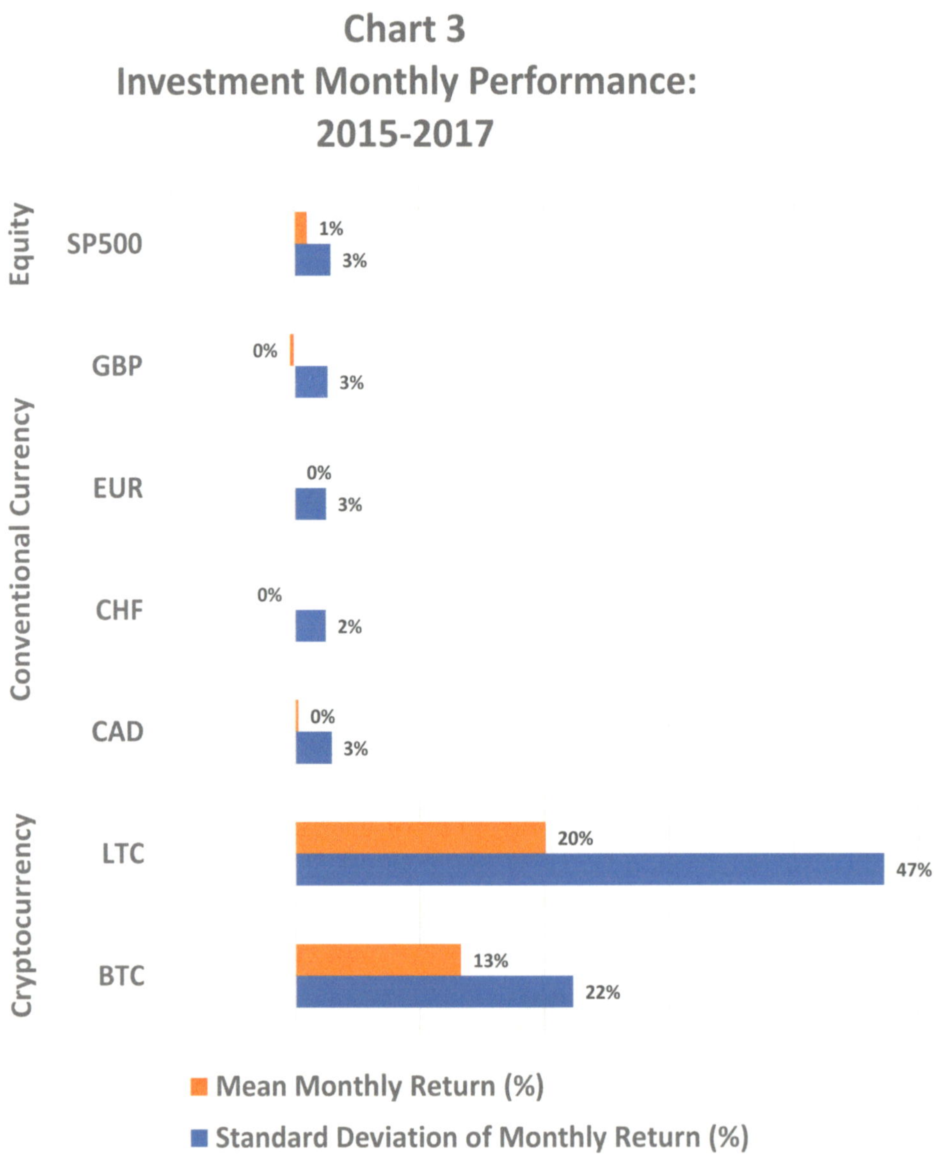


**Chart 2.** Major Cryptocurrency vs Conventional Currency Risk-Return Performance: 2017.

largest conventional currencies, and the SP500 stock index. The four largest cryptocurrencies by market capitalization (as of the end of 2017) are the BTC, LTC, DASH, and XMR. The four dominant conventional currencies consist of the British pound (GBP), the Euro (EUR), the Swiss franc (CHF), and the Canadian dollar (CAD). **Chart 2** presents the mean monthly returns and standard deviations of return for the 2017 calendar year for selected investments across different investment classes. Again, note how the risk and return measures for the cryptocurrencies dwarf those of other conventional currencies, as well as those of the SP500.

For the sake of a brief, but more focused and isolated contrast, consider the returns and standard deviations of return solely on the Bitcoin, the British Pound, and the SP500 below for 2017:

While the Bitcoin return is roughly 17 times that of the SP500, its risk in terms of the standard deviation of monthly return is also commensurately higher. Note that the SP500 and the British pound are relatively sedate investment alternatives when compared to the Bitcoin, and the Bitcoin is the most conservative investment alternative among the cryptocurrencies.

The relationship between risk and return across these investments in different asset classes can be displayed in the form of a line graph (see **Graph 2**). Again, observe the positive relationship between risk and return. Moreover, note that the positive risk-return relationship is clearly present within the cryptocurrencies themselves, with the most well-known cryptocurrency, the Bitcoin, demonstrating the least volatility and lowest average return among the cryptocurrencies displayed.

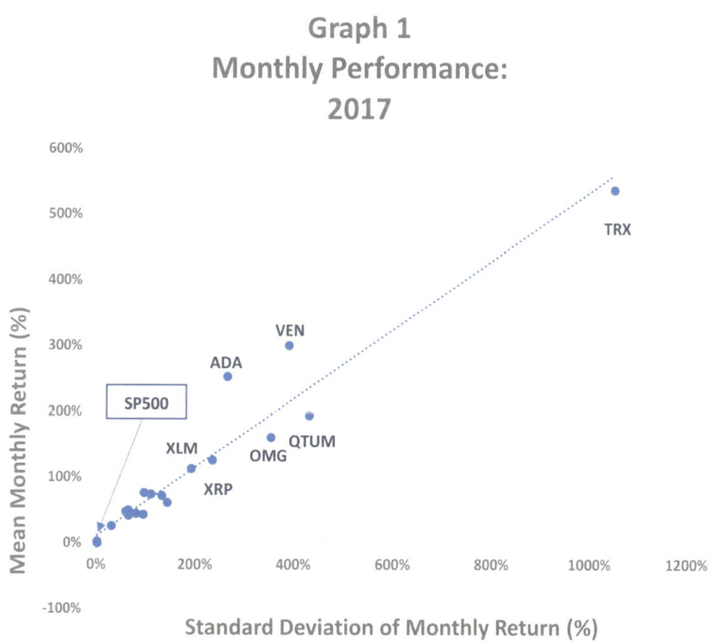


**Graph 2.** Mean monthly return (%) among investment group alternatives: 2017.

## 4. Long-term cryptocurrency performance comparison

The potential sustainability of the risk-return pattern offered by cryptocurrencies is examined by observing a longer period of performance. The risk and return of cryptocurrencies, conventional currencies, and the SP500 stock index are presented for a 3-year period, 2015–2017 (refer to **Chart 3**). Since the Bitcoin (BTC) and Litecoin (LTC) were the only cryptocurrencies trading throughout the 2015–2017 time period, only these two cryptocurrencies are included in this long-term performance compared to more conventional investments.[7]

Note that while the differences in performance between cryptocurrencies and other investments for this 3-year period are somewhat less striking than for the explosive year 2017, there still exists an enormous performance gap. Returns on the two cryptocurrencies (BTC and LTC) are roughly 10 times those of the comparative investments, and likewise, the levels of risk (i.e., standard deviation of monthly returns) are comparably higher.

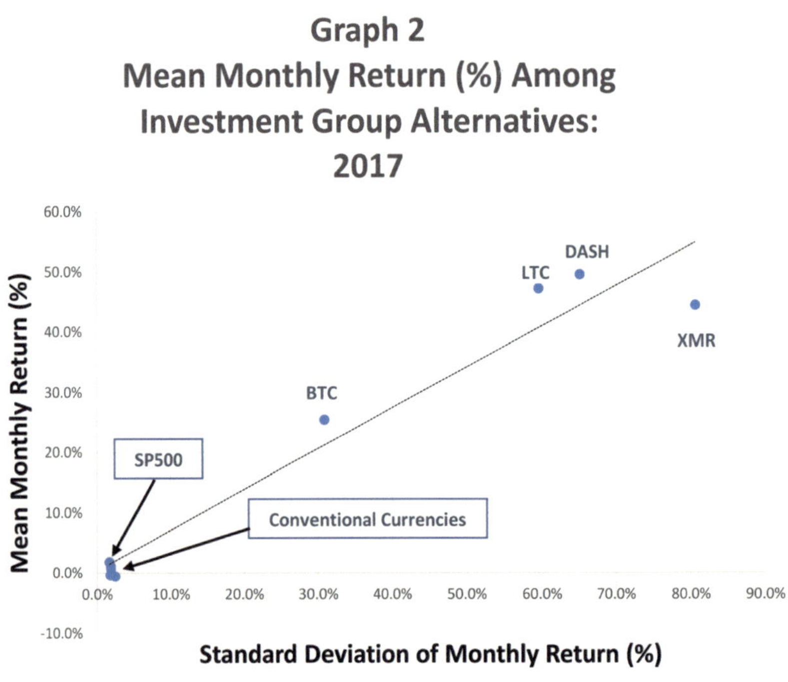


**Chart 3.** Investment monthly performance: 2015-2017.

[7]The Bitcoin and Litecoin began publicly trading on February 5, 2013.

http://dx.doi.org/10.5772/intechopen.80397

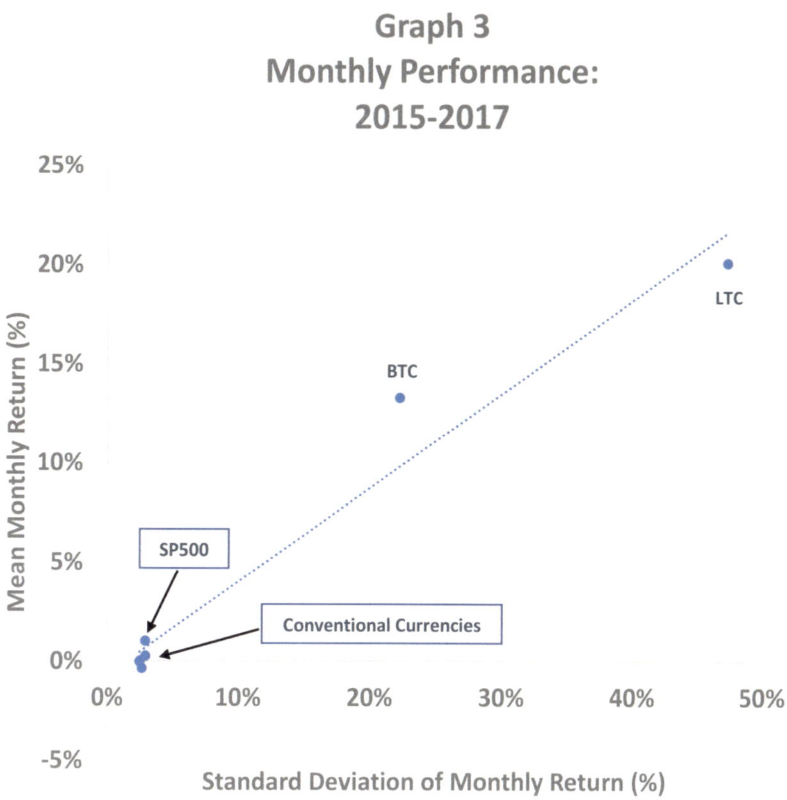


**Graph 3.** Monthly performance: 2015-2017.

The long-term performance contrast is also presented in the form of a line graph (see **Graph 3**). Note that the two cryptocurrencies (BTC and LTC) display risk and return values that are high multiples of those of the SP500 or conventional currencies.

## 5. Summary

Whether examining performance for the explosive year 2017, or for a longer period, cryptocurrencies offer another alternative to investors that involves considerably higher risk and commensurately higher return than typical of conventional investments. Compared to the high average returns and standard deviations of return of cryptocurrencies, investment in conventional currencies or the stock market (SP500) appears relatively sedate by comparison. Cryptocurrency returns have averaged a level equal to roughly 20 or more times those of conventional currencies or equity investment. Although cryptocurrencies offer the attraction of enormously high returns, cryptocurrency investment is also accompanied by substantially higher risk.

## Author details

Mike Cudd[1], Kristen Ritterbush[2], Marcelo Eduardo[1]* and Chris Smith[1]

*Address all correspondence to: eduardo@mc.edu

1 School of Business, Mississippi College, Clinton, MS, USA

2 School of Business, University of Arkansas, Fayetteville, AR, USA

## References

[1] Maese V, Avery A, Naftalis B, Wink S, Valdez, Yvette D. Cryptocurrency: A primer. Banking Law Journal. 2016;**133**:468-471

[2] Antoncic M. Bitcoin and other cryptocurrencies: Tulip mania or the next amazon? Journal of Risk Management in Financial Institutions. 2017/2018;**11**(1):4-9

[3] Li X. The technology and economic determinants of cryptocurrency exchange rates: The case of the Bitcoin. Decision Support Systems. 2017;**95**:49-60

[4] Harwick C. Cryptocurrency and the problem of intermediation. The Independent Review. 2016;**20**(4):569-588

[5] Briere M, Oosterlink K, Szafarz A. Virtual currency, tangible return: Portfolio diversification with Bitcoin. Journal of Asset Management. 2015;**16**(6):365-373

[6] Corbet S, Meegan A, Larkin C, Lucey B, Yarovaya L. Exploring the dynamic relationships between cryptocurrencies and other financial assets. Economic Letters. 2018;**165**:28-34

[7] Chowdhury S. Is bitcoin the "Paris Hilton" of the currency world? Or are the early investors onto something that will make them rich? Journal of Investing. 2016;**25**(1):64-72

[8] Phillip A, Chan J, Peiris S. A new look at cryptocurrencies. Economic Letters. 2018;**163**:6-9

[9] Brauneis A, Mestel R. Price discovery of cryptocurrencies: Bitcoin and beyond. Economic Letters. 2018;**165**:58-61

[10] Gkillas K, Katsiampa P. An application of extreme value theory to cryptocurrencies. Economic Letters. 2018;**164**:109-111

[11] https://www.wsj.com/articles/sec-launches-cryptocurrency-probe-1519856266

[12] https://www.wsj.com/articles/new-york-pushes-crypto-exchanges-for-more-transparency-1523980862

[13] https://www.wsj.com/articles/u-s-regulators-demand-trading-data-from-bitcoin-exchanges-in-manipulation-probe-1528492835?mod=djemalertNEWS

[14] https://www.cnbc.com/2018/01/10/buffett-says-cyrptocurrencies-will-almost-certainly-end-badly.html

[15] https://en.wikipedia.org/wiki/Ethereum

[16] https://en.wikipedia.org/wiki/History_of_bitcoin

[17] https://finance.yahoo.com/

Section 3

# Impact of Cryptocurrencies in Gaming

Chapter 4

# Cryptocurrencies in the Ludic Economies: The Case of Contemporary Game Cultures

Leonardo José Mataruna-dos-Santos and
Vanissa Wanick

Additional information is available at the end of the chapter

http://dx.doi.org/10.5772/intechopen.80950

**Abstract**

Games have their own economic models. Today, players can not only collect digital currencies, but they can also use real currencies to buy virtual goods. Business models in games such as freemium and in-app purchases, for example, sustain this structure. Within this context, there is also the expansion of models outside the game realm like eSports, which happens in the form of tournaments. With this, there is constant exchange of value that emerges from games, which could also include the use of cryptocurrencies. In this chapter, we give an overview of the current state of the art of economic models within games and eSports. The current chapter aims to situate and analyse the application of these business models derived from games, e-sport and the future of ludic economies.

**Keywords:** games, cryptocurrencies, ludic economies, eSports, economic models

## 1. Introduction

Games and eSports market are increasing every year, including the mobile sector that is competing directly with the traditional platforms and consoles. According to [1], by 2020, the eSports industry will reach 1.65 billion US dollars. Similarly, a study by [2] on the global games market forecasts that '2.3 billion gamers across the globe will spend $137.9 billion on games in 2018. Digital game revenues will take 91% of the global market with $125.3 billion'. The same trend can also be observed in the video game consumer market performance, with an increase of value from downloadable contents (DLC) in comparison to usual package models (see **Figure 1**). Most of the time, this revenue is earned through the selling of virtual goods within games.

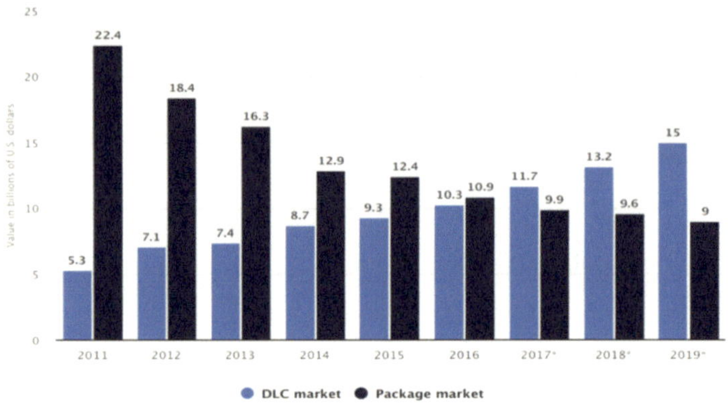


**Figure 1.** Video game consumer market value worldwide from 2011 to 2019, by distribution type (in billion US dollars) [1].

With technological advances, game developers and designers have found an opportunity to explore the business of virtual goods in order to increase their revenue stream, particularly through in-app purchases (IAP). One example is the freemium model [3]. For example, in the mobile game *Clash of Clans*, players can buy 'time' to have their goods ready for battle (e.g. players can pay to get their house built quicker), relying on players' impatience to progress in the game [4]. No wonder, *Clash of Clans*' creators earn more than 15 million per day using this game-business model [5]. Considering this, it is possible to understand the intersection between economics and games in two ways: one as a game structure (e.g. collecting coins, accumulation of goods) and another through microtransactions (e.g. buying time or goods to progress in the game). This opens the door to possible problems that could affect the player experience. For example, players might buy their way up in the leaderboard using real money, or they might buy power-ups to win battles inside the game or even use cheat codes to have as much virtual money as they can. In fact, some websites offer online auctions for power-ups of some games following the tendencies of online auctions. Actions were very were very popular in the early days of Internet commerce, but today online sellers mostly use posted prices [6]. This is not an official market developed by the gaming industry; however, there is an emerging and potential economy around power-ups (selling and buying), with physical currencies and/or cryptocurrencies that require attention. It notes that complex games, especially massively multiplayer online role-playing games (MMORPGs), contain narrative and mechanisms that mimic real economic activities, such as production, trade and consumption [7]. Those factors can contribute to this 'emerging economy' using the auction system.

Virtual goods are not the only venue that could be explored in games business models. Since there are many transactions involved in games, this could also open the opportunity to explore cryptocurrencies. It mentions the gamification techniques as a strategy used to incentivize participation in mobile crowd-sensing applications that can be conveyed by cryptocurrencies [8]. The effectiveness of cryptocurrency gamification schemes depends considerably on a large set of interrelated factors from community-related (number of participants) to cultural or motivational factors [9]. According to [10], if societies want to adopt cryptocurrencies, it is necessary to think differently about past sources, investments and revenues (including sustainability).

Cryptocurrencies are decentralised currencies that rely on cryptography to secure their safety and trust; these are powerful mathematical protocols (e.g. blockchain) that avoid 'cheating' or fraud [11]. Blockchain is a decentralised transaction and data management technology developed first for *Bitcoin* [12]. The authors [13] reinforce that the term cryptocurrency can be seen either as currency or as a 'synthetic commodity money', which 'resembles fiat money in having no nonmonetary value (but also) resembles commodity money in being not just contingently but absolutely scarce' [14]. Online and social media factors are currently related to the time intervals of cryptocurrency prices; thus it was observed 'that cryptocurrencies are prone to experience intervals of bubble-like price growth' [15].

One of the most popular cryptocurrencies is *Bitcoin* that dominates the cryptocurrency markets and presents researchers with a rich source of real-time transactional data [16]. *Bitcoin* is a decentralised currency [11] that relies on peer-to-peer (P2P) cash system and network consensus. Thus, cryptocurrencies are 'agreed' currencies that rely on algorithms to be trustable. The mechanics of cryptocurrencies like *Bitcoin* are similar to a game. Metaphorically speaking, mining could be the effort that one has in the game to progress and the currency is the virtual reward that could be exchanged for something else. With that, games and money have a lot in common. For instance, cryptocurrencies allow individuals to have fun while earning money [17]. This association is part of a rewarding experience, which is a core mechanic in games. Hence, like in a game, 'real' money becomes a reward. Considering this, with many advances on technology and games, there is an opportunity to explore the application of cryptocurrencies in games. How can designers and developers implement cryptocurrencies in their game business models? What are the main characteristics of cryptocurrencies in games? What are the main challenges? In light of these questions, this chapter aims to understand the features and current state of the art that dwells within the profitable market of games and eSports.

## 2. Ludic economies, economic models and virtual goods

The term ludic economies is a critical reflection on the parallels between play and economic models [18]. These relationships could be understood through comparisons towards 'capitalist' thinking through the accumulation of resources. The 'capitalisation' refers to the action of collecting points, coins, digital currency or other incoming, just for getting rich or to enhance the score. The 'monetisation' refers to the points or money collected in the game which can be used to buy items such as clothes, guns, powers and others that will provide more power or capacity to collect more money or incomings. According to [19], there are three revenue models to consider: Freemium is 'coined through the contraction of "free" and "premium". It refers to a revenue model which enables consumers to have a certain product or service for free and getting revenue from additional features provided, usually to a small percentage of the user base'; premium is 'basing income on a transaction with a given price which is agreed, and many times paid for, prior to getting the product or service'; and subscription is the 'model based on periodic payments in return for a periodic or continuous service and/or product deliveries'. These models have been used historically in the video game industry, and, theoretically, they would fit personal computer video games and the specific genre of Multiplayer Online Battle Arena (MOBA). Some game companies are studying ways to implement cryptocurrencies for payments of the three revenue models.

A classic example of 'capitalisation' occurs in *SuperMario Bros* (Nintendo®), in which players need to collect coins while jumping and fighting enemies. Also, in the classic board game *Monopoly*, players start with a specific amount of money and then buy houses, charge rent and upgrade their belongings. These models are inherent in the mechanics of these games. Although in *SuperMario Bros* players cannot 'buy' anything in the game, there is still an accumulation of 'capital' that could be traded to extra health, new avatar clothing or others. This helps to create an in-game economy or a micro-economy inside the game, supported by game mechanics and player psychology. Considering this, mechanics that might favour currency exchange are object collection through accumulation, trading systems (with virtual or real money) and mastery through accumulation (e.g. players could collect a bunch of abilities/ power-ups). In fact, Nintendo® also created a new version of *SuperMario* for iPhone and Android, called *SuperMario Run*. In the new game for mobile, the personage collects coins to exchange for elements in the game. It is available in the same game, the 'Toad Rally Ticket', a kind of currency to exchange for the opportunity to play special phases or mini-rally. You may have to pay one 'Rally' ticket to enter a race, but you can earn back what you paid, plus more, if you win a 'Rally'. In the game *Need for Speed* (2015), the player can collect points, convert it into money and use it to upgrade the car before the race. In this case, the concept of monetarism according to the definition of [20], who present an 'economic theory based on the view that the quantity of money is the main determinant of money incomes', is applicable.

Remembering the precursor games, since beginning the Mario Bros® arcade version in 1983, designed by Shigeru Miyamoto and Gunpei Yokoi, the same developers of *Donkey Kong* (first arcade where the character *Mario* appears as coadjutant, early 1980s) used basic concepts of capitalisation described by [21], when the personage collects coins in the route, breaking boxes or eliminating adversaries [22]. However, Nintendo® launched in 1985 the platform for video games and since then used concepts in more than 70 versions of the *Super Mario* series, such as *Odyssey*, *Galaxy*, *World* and others. With this, games would have their own economic model, be it using real or digital money. For instance, with just a click, players can buy a very valuable item in the game by just using their credit card. [19] comments:

> *Paying customers are offered either to progress at a faster pace or a certain advantage also available to non-playing users willing to invest enough time into the game. In light of this, some games function with a dual currency system. Hard currency is obtained only by putting money into the game and soft currency is only obtained through time spent in game or logons (or though other mechanism such as number of wins). Offers for sale can be priced then in one or both of these currencies, determining then what can be bought with money, with time or with either one or the other* (p.6) [19].

For instance, 'pay to win' is an option that can be applied for cheating or winning, escaping hard stages, collecting more sources or enhancing the revenue. For example, in the game *Candy Crush*, the user can buy power-ups to destroy barriers in hard stages or extra movements and additional life, to follow to the next stage increasing the revenue. The game also provides free power-ups in different stages for promoting a power-up testing. For multiplayer games, as player(s) versus player(s) (PvP), it is not ethically accepted in the western countries [19]. That action provides a customer engagement and a transformation in the consumer behaviour of users. A kind of power-up dependence is generated for further improvement of performance, promoting a consumer who is continuously engaged and the usage of currency conversion for digital or virtual money.

### 2.1. Virtual goods in games

Virtual goods are 'in-game objects' that players can use only in the game, like avatar clothing styles, power-ups, extra lives, weapons, places and time (p1) [23]. Virtual goods can be bought by real money or in-game currency. For example, in the popular farm game *Farmville*, players can trade in the game, earn money from their farm and use this money to buy goods, but they can also buy these goods using real money. The willingness to buy a virtual good will then depend on the player. For instance, [24] has found when players have fun with the game, they would be less keen to buy virtual goods. On the other hand, if players play the game with more frequency, they tend to buy more virtual goods. Thus, purchasing virtual goods in games can be subjective. Also, in the same study, the author found that social interaction influences people's intention to buy virtual goods [24]. It is also important to note that games are rewarding systems and game currencies reflect those rewards. For example, you can only get coins in *SuperMario Bros* if you jump in the right position. Therefore, it is possible to say that virtual goods are in-game rewards, which could be a new character ability, new clothing, new scenarios/arenas/environments and objects that could be purchased by in-game currency or real money (through in-app purchases).

### 2.2. Cryptocurrencies in games

Cryptocurrencies are currencies supported by agreed protocols [11]. Thus, in a game, a cryptocurrency is a currency that allows players to make exchanges inside the game, which may also involve 'real' money. *The Sims* is a great example of using virtual money inside a game. The game itself mimics the real world; players can go to work, earn their salary and buy objects for their house. However, according to [25] players may wish to cheat in the game to get as much money as they can. In fact, a simple code in the game can give more than 1000 *simoleons* to the player 'for free'. With that, becoming a 'cheater' in the game can be easy and acceptable since the codes are public. Thus, how to protect the dignity of the currency? How to prevent cheating? In sports games, there is no cheat code list. However, on the perspective of [26] in games like FIFA, developed by EA for mobile platforms, there is a constant use of in-app purchases inside the game. This suggests that if a player would like to have more power-ups, he/she could pay for it. Thus, what cryptocurrencies and games have in common is their rewarding system. The difference between them is on the path towards earning this currency and the player's values and intentions, since while playing games, players tend to exercise their values [27]. This means that if players feel like cheating and if the game allows this behaviour, they might do it. Thus, how can we make sure this currency is trustable?

Regarding cryptocurrency and games, it is possible to mention strong market correlations between *Bitcoin* and other gaming currencies. Some currencies in the blockchain carry in their names the terminology 'games' or description in their profiles and using the games as principles in the market. Using *Bitcoin* as comparative parameter, it is possible to observe some examples in the market (see **Figures 2** and **3**).

[28] remembered that 'gaming cryptocurrencies could change the face and economies of gaming and they are growing on an industry-wide scale to new all-time highs every day'.

| | | | |
|---|---|---|---|
| GameCredits (GAME) | $1.19 USD (19.47%)<br>0.00015585 BTC (16.28%) | | Cryptocurrency Ranking 155 |
| **Market Cap** | **Volume (24h)** | **Circulating Supply** | **Max Supply** |
| $76557127 USD<br>10030 BTC | $1160790 USD<br>152.08 BTC | 64355352 GAME | 84000000 GAME |

| | | | |
|---|---|---|---|
| MonaCoin (MONA) | $3.32 USD (0.69%)<br>0.00043452 BTC (-2.00%) | | Cryptocurrency Ranking 74 |
| **Market Cap** | **Volume (24h)** | **Circulating Supply** | **Max Supply** |
| $198895385 USD<br>26058 BTC | $861695 USD<br>112.89 BTC | 59970025 MONA | |

| | | | |
|---|---|---|---|
| Game.com (GTC) | $0.135197 USD (5.99%)<br>0.00001774 BTC (3.34%)<br>0.00022190 ETH (2.18%) | | Cryptocurrency Ranking 153 |
| **Market Cap** | **Volume (24h)** | **Circulating Supply** | **Max Supply** |
| $81587500 USD<br>10703 BTC<br>133908 ETH | $2258850 USD<br>296.34 BTC<br>3707 ETH | 603471233 GTC | 2000000000 GTC |

**Figure 2.** Comparative market of gaming currencies using Bitcoin and USD as references. (Data extracted from Coinmarketcap on June 5, 2018) [30].

As mentioned by [29], it is possible to observe that although the Bitcoin market grows rapidly, there are still some doubts whether cryptocurrencies are a fad or a more efficient way to exchange goods (and money).

**Figure 3.** Two years' chart comparison between GameCredits, Bitcoin and US Dollar [30].

In the game perspective, it is possible to observe as shown in **Figure 3** the 2-year behaviour of *GameCredits* while comparing its value in US dollar and Bitcoin. **Figure 4** is a visual impression of the trend in stock prices measured on daily closing records. The fluctuations in the prices are shown during the period from June 2017 to June 2018. The two estimated trend lines are showing a 3-month moving average and a linear trend, respectively. In simple words they are showing average movement during the period. The behaviour in June 2017 and during December 2017 to January 2018 is abnormal and showing unusual rise compared to the overall fluctuations during 2017–2018. Except these two points, the overall trend was stable.

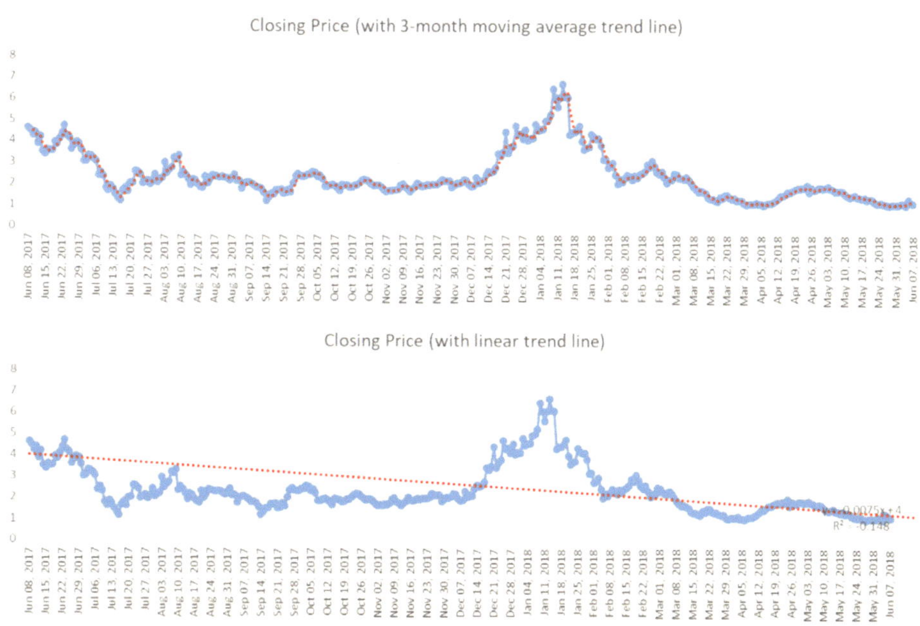


**Figure 4.** GameCredits' stock price trend 2017–2018. Source: developed by the authors based on the market data [30].

The linear trend prediction for the rest of the months in 2018 is showing the similar expected price level. The estimated linear regression line is Y = 4–0.0075 t. The goodness of linear fit ($R^2$) is not very strong due to the seasonal nature of the data. Therefore the 3-month moving average provides better forecasting in this type of fluctuations. In **Figure 3**, the period from August 2016 to September 2017, the variables are highly correlated. Thereafter the variables seem to move in opposite directions. In **Figure 4**, it seems to have a downward trend with a high volatility in the period analysed.

### 2.2.1. *Blockchain in the cryptogames*

Cryptocurrencies have structures that are similar to a game. The same principle is applied in both: people are rewarded by their actions, and they can use the rewards to buy goods. One of the first 'cryptogames' that use similarities with *Bitcoin* is the *Huntercoin*. Using the blockchain universe to collect coins, *Huntercoin* presents an element P2P combat to fight over resources. This can be termed as human (or AI) mining, and the competition which has gotten more difficult over time can be called a human (or AI) difficulty level [31]. Using a cryptographically secure technology, decentralised and innovative, Huntercoin was released in February 2014 as a live experimental test to see how blockchain technology could handle full on-game worlds. Huntercoin proved this concept well and is still in development today. In the cryptogame market, a diversity of cryptocurrencies are available, represented by the ticker symbol as presented in the world cloud, **Figure 5**—sides 'A' and 'B'. The cryptogame shares the principles with other cryptogames in the blockchain perspective, such as *Namecoin* (NMC); *Spells of Genesis* (a mobile game that is a mix of a trading card game (TCG), bringing in deck collection and strategy, along with arcade-style gaming aspect); *Rare Pepe Party* (RAREPEPEPRTY) that is a TCG in development with role-playing game (RPG) elements, inspired by *Hearthstone* and the *Pokemon* series; and others. Ref. [32] mentioned Chimaera (CHI) is one of the first and only second-generation game coin. Different than other gaming cryptocurrencies, CHI primarily focuses on asset registry and trade, creating an ecosystem in which games are built and played directly on the blockchain with two possibilities of cryptocurrencies: *GameCredits* (GAME) and *MobileGO* (MGO) [32].

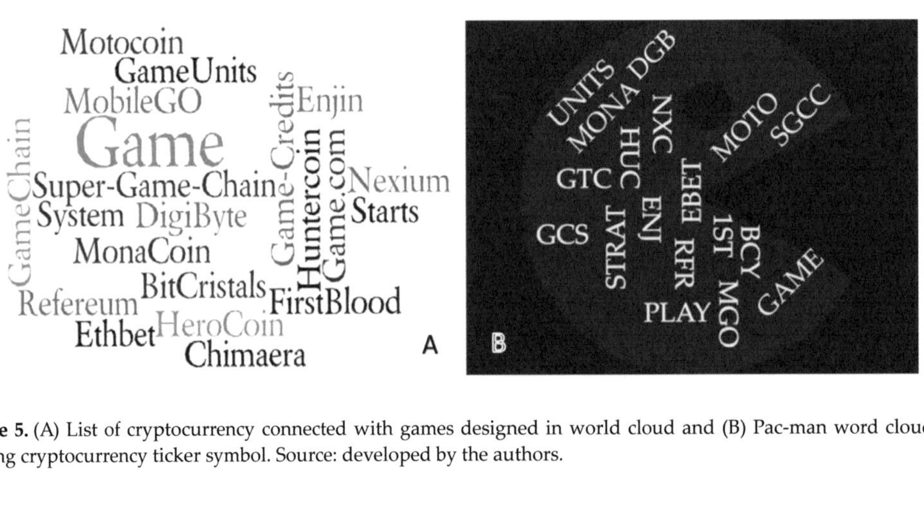


**Figure 5.** (A) List of cryptocurrency connected with games designed in world cloud and (B) Pac-man word cloud of gaming cryptocurrency ticker symbol. Source: developed by the authors.

Ref. [33] mentioned that 'six months after the *CryptoKitties* craze, momentum continues to build behind blockchain-based games and non-fungible crypto collectibles'. The AEON Foundation, the blockchain game company and publisher of the Crypto Alpaca crypto-pet game, announced that it had secured USD 5 M in seed funding for the development of its distributed blockchain video-gaming platform. The Crypto Alpaca is based on the reality game in which players collect, breed and trade unique alpacas, the South American animal (similar to a llama) that is the original mascot of bitcoin; the game has logged more than 200,000 registrations since launch, comments [33]. Players are able to collect rewards and increase the value of their alpacas by feeding and shearing them and doing other activities. It is a new moment for the industry that probably will associate sooner the conventional platforms with the blockchain, mixing the real world and virtual actions. This is a huge opportunity for businesses and markets to expand their models. The video game industry is a sector worth $100 bil [34].

Observed data has four types of trend known as secular, seasonal, cyclical and random. Various statistical techniques are used to separate these trends and fit the best trend line according to the true nature of the data. Observed data in **Figure 4** is seasonally affected and fluctuates persistently from year to year in quarterly stretched intervals. Therefore, the trend measured on the constant value of $\beta$ is not appropriate statistics to predict in the recent future. Separating seasonal trends on the bases of 3-months moving average predicts based on the average value of 3 periods and moves along with the observed data.

### 2.3. eSports and economic models

The term 'eSports' (or electronic sports) is a derivation of the conventional sports; thus, ethical and educational values are part of the play action of users. Recently, eSports are following one tendency to become part of sport mega-events, such as the Asian Games, the Olympic Games and the FIFA World Cup [35]. Commenting on the eSports and gaming, [28] describe both as one of the biggest industries today, and in 2017, there were about 2.2 billion gamers across the globe that are expected to generate $108.9 billion in-game revenues.

There is a large discussion if eSports could be considered a 'real' sport and if players are 'athletes'. eSports are sports since they share the same type of mechanics as a traditional sport like football [36]. eSports have fans, spectators, leagues, teams, structures and financial support (e.g. sponsorships). There is a huge opportunity for companies to sponsor players and teams. In fact, eSports have been considered as an Olympic game modality, and its first event was the eGames showcase that took place in Brazil [37]. The Rio de Janeiro eGames Showcase 2016, launched as part of this week's London Games Festival and the Rio Olympics Games, offered medals and national pride rather than cash prizes for the winners. Ref. [38] comments that eSports 'will be an official medal sport at the 2022 Asian Games in China, in the boldest step yet towards mainstream recognition of competitive gaming'. The same author highlighted that the Olympic Council of Asia (OCA) announced a partnership with Alisports, the sports arm of Chinese online retail giant Alibaba, to introduce eSports as a demonstration sport at next year's games in Indonesia 2018, with full-fledged inclusion in the official sporting programme at the Hangzhou Games in 2022. Some people still have the idea that eSport is just for fun, but it is not. This is a powerful market and businesses should pay attention to it.

Ref. [38] refreshed that the Alibaba Sports Group announced a $150 m investment in 2016 with the International eSports Federation (IeSF), the South Korea-based federation that has long campaigned for the inclusion of competitive gaming in the Olympic Games. "It put forth more than $14.5m to organize the World Electronic Sports Games in China's Changzhou province, where roughly 60,000 players from 120 countries and regions competed for a $5.5m purse in 2018".

According to [2, 39], FIFA 2018 is one of the most watched games on Twitch and YouTube Gaming. In April 2018, the total prize pools for console eSports events reached $2.5 million, which is the double the amount awarded in the first quarter of 2017. Those data show that the game market is bigger than just selling consoles, games, accessories, power-ups and gadgets. Nowadays, the game industry manages the other slice of the market, such as the social media platforms, betting companies, mega-events, sport consumer and identity, television rights and e-channels that manage viewership hours, market share, top tournaments and titles and investments [40–43]. Ref. [39] comments that 20 M of console eSports hours was watched on Twitch and YouTube Gaming between January and April 2018, representing 4.6% of the total games broadcasted. It is demonstrated in the 95% year-on-year growth of viewership of major tournaments on Twitch and put eSports in third position of top console genres with 21% of the market.

Betting companies also use eSports; however, both big traditional sportsbooks and newer start-ups are competing for space. It is possible to find examples of virtual or physical betting companies such as: bet365, betway esport, unibet, #OneHash – are possible to find virtual or physical, such as bet365, betway esport, unibet, and #OneHash—using *Bitcoin*, mr green, gg.bet, Betsson, and Betsafe – that is a sponsor of extreme sports events like *Redbull* and hosts the yearly Gumball 3000 car race across continents. This industry uses a real money, digital currency, cryptocurrency or 'fake currency' to gather and compose the most interesting contemporary eSports sportsbooks and move the game economy.

The virtual economies created within massively multiplayer online role-playing games (MMORPGs) often blur the line between real and virtual worlds. The result is often seen as an unwanted interaction between the real and virtual economies by the players and the provider of the virtual world. This practice (economy interaction) is mostly seen in this genre of games. The two seem to come hand in hand with even the earliest MMORPGs such as *Ultima Online* having this kind of trade, real money for virtual things.

The importance of having a working virtual economy within an MMORPG is increasing as they develop. A sign of this is the CCP Games hiring the first real-life economist for its MMORPG 'Eve Online' to assist and analyse the virtual economy and production within this game. The results of this interaction between the virtual world, and our real economy, is the future of the gaming industry.

## 3. Models and applications of cryptocurrencies in games and eSports

Since ludic economies rely on economic dynamics and the way the game is designed, we have synthesised the main models that drive cryptocurrencies in games and eSports into a combination of virtual goods, game mechanics, values, economic models and currencies (see **Figure 6**). This combination of elements reflects the interdisciplinarity and relationship of several elements that are both derived from economics and design. Thus, in order to understand the economic aspect of businesses of games and ludic economies, we have also included four models:

Market model. The market model is a concept that explains how prices of the various items are determined in the game (or game market place). It explains how demand and supply forces interact with each other and settle down the prices. Whether it is virtual or real money, they are scarce, and the player has to put efforts to get it [44]. Thus, the market model functions as a holistic approach that guides ludic economies.

Consumer behaviour. Consumer (or player) behaviour reflects the factors that play an important role in the decision-making of consumers (or players) in order to buy any item or product. For example, there are many factors that can influence the player's purchases of in-game virtual goods, including fun and social interactions [24]. Furthermore, consumer behaviour has a strong relationship to what the game offers to players. For example, time left in the game, or the position of player in the game (or status), influences the player's perceptions and willingness to buy virtual goods [42, 43].

Income model. Income model is a construct that explains the variables that determine the level of income of the player. It is the average level of income that a player maintains to achieve strategic depth in the game. It further explains how psychological factors of the player act to change the income generating behaviour [45-47] of the player act to change the income generating behaviour [45–47].

Price strategy. Price strategy is a form of economic theory. In games, it can be related to how different players in oligopolistic market conditions are maintaining certain degree of rivalry. It can also include how players design their game strategies to win economic victory that ultimately will help them to win the game [7, 44, 48].

The four models mentioned are part of the drivers of the other elements that mediate the use of cryptocurrencies in games and eSports. As illustrated in **Figure 6**, price strategy, consumer behaviour, market model and income model permeate the other five drivers of the applications of cryptocurrencies in ludic economies. For example, if considering values (e.g. individual values, cultural values, etc.), consumer behaviour could function as the main influencer of game systems. Thus, in the next section, we introduce and discuss the main applications of cryptocurrencies in games and eSports with examples in two scenarios: eSports and (digital) games.

### 3.1. eSports

#### 3.1.1. *Tournaments*

For eSports tournaments, the consumer is the spectator, who pays to watch the 'match' in an arena. From the consumer behaviour perspective, spectators find value in buying tickets to watch the game being played by professional players. As a tournament or event, eSports is a very valuable market. There are many opportunities for brands to sponsor professional players and games. Some managers are offering sponsorship for teams and players via Internet-booming opportunities. Comparing with other conventional sports, it is easy to find companies and businessmen available for investing in this sector. The type of the game, the place and the

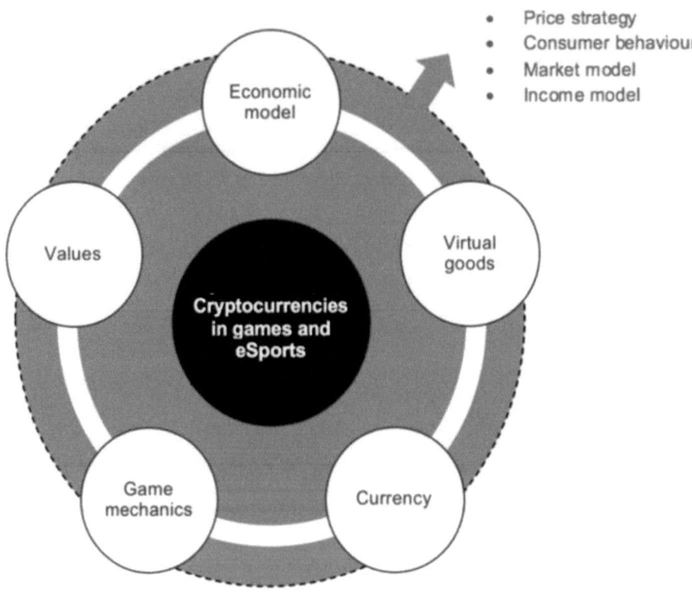


**Figure 6.** Cryptocurrencies in games and eSports. Source: developed by the authors.

prizes are some of the aspects responsible for attracting players and spectators. With this, the consumer identity is developed based on the teams, 'athletes' and the events [49].

### *3.1.2. Broadcasting*

When players are broadcasting their gameplay, spectators can also participate, interacting directly with the events, players and market according to the rules and structure of the competition. For example, *Youtube Gaming* and *Twitch* have forums that allow users to share their thoughts with other spectators. In a more participatory scenario, spectators could use platforms like *Microsoft Mixer* to give hints and comments to the player [[50, 49]. In the case of using virtual goods, spectators could get points to buy goods in the game for the players. Also, spectators could get points by watching and commenting on players' performance. These points could be exchanged to real goods (e.g., pizza, drinks, etc.) or virtual goods (e.g. unlock more content, etc.). Players could get more currency by counting the amount of people who are watching them play. The commercialization of eSports is a new opportunity for the game market that can be associated with new digital currencies [51]. Cryptocurrencies could be employed in this context in order to aid the exchange between points collected by watching other players and real goods, such as food or other commodities. As players and spectators interact more often through digital tools, the cryptocurrency could earn more value in its own stock market.

## 3.2. Games

The biggest market for games (in particular mobile games) is the utilisation of in-app purchases and the commercialisation of virtual goods. This can be employed in any digital game. Thus,

| Model | eSports | Games |
|---|---|---|
| Market model | Spectators can buy goods in the arena and merchandising; spectators can sponsor players and collect points | In-app purchases, freemium, virtual goods |
| Consumer behaviour | Identity with teams; fan culture, community | Identity, ownership, competition, collaboration, community |
| Income model | Brands could sponsor players; might depend on the place; points could be exchanged to virtual/real goods | Players pay for virtual goods that could be exchanged to real/virtual goods; players could exchange their virtual/real goods through the game |
| Price strategy | Depends on the demand and place | Could be more fixed; depends on competitors |

**Table 1.** Comparison between eSports and games models using cryptocurrencies.

for digital games, the market model depends on the game mechanics. For example, if players want to buy assets for their game character, then they will purchase them. Thus, the main concern for these games is to match the mechanics to this model and build a digital access to these virtual goods. For players, it could be that they want to buy specific clothes for their characters in order to resemble their own appearance. Thus, the need to buy virtual goods might have a relationship with the player's preference. As [40] mentioned, some assets and specific characters might carry an advantage in the game, depending on the character's ability and the game challenge. Therefore, there is an opportunity to generate a need for new gaming assets, creating a high demand for this type of commodity (or virtual goods). Another opportunity for games is the integration with emerging technologies such as virtual reality (VR) and augmented reality (AR). For instance, mobile games like *Pokemon Go* could merge the digital market model with the physical, generating new demands and interactions between players [52]. For example, players could play a mobile game and pay for a virtual good that will only appear in their screen. Ref. [53] mentioned that brands like IKEA are already using this type of technology to help consumers to visualise the position of furniture in their own homes. Games could use a similar strategy to allow players to visualise and have the feeling of ownership upon their virtual goods. Also, players could be able to share their own virtual goods and with that promote a more decentralised model, which could be supported by cryptocurrencies (**Table 1**).

## 4. Final remarks

In this chapter, we have analysed and discussed the current market and economic opportunities for games and eSports. For that, we explored the models and applications of cryptocurrencies in games and eSports and how economic models may emerge from interactions between players, spectators and games. From freemium models to betting, games have many mechanisms that are similar to our capitalist society, mimicking systems of trade, capital accumulation (e.g. same as game points) and exchange. For instance, [54] commented that the stock exchange is minting millionaires who know how to play the market every day, just like a game. Thanks to online trading with the BAWSAQ stock exchange, it is possible to lay it all on the line by betting on a stock. The problem of approaching games as an economy is that gambling and betting can become real risks for players. For example, gaming structures like *Loot Boxes* (e.g. players buy 'boxes' of virtual goods without knowing what is inside) can become a similar form of gambling, and in fact, there are countries in the globe that consider this as gambling [55]. Thus, it is possible that cryptocurrencies in the gaming environment should consider ethical and psychological effects on consumers, which may include issues around local regulations.

As mentioned in this chapter, games can embed their own stock market. The stock market in the game *Grand Theft Auto V* (GTA V) operates with the same goal as real-life stock trading; in the game, players can buy products with low prices and sell them with higher prices, in order to turn them into profit. The value of stocks is affected by various things including story progress, in-game purchases and other players [56]. It is expected that the same model could be applied to the value of cryptocurrency in the next edition of the game. Cryptocurrencies could also act as a medium of exchange of goods and services in-game (like convenience stores). Multiplayer games could also allow collective team mining in reward of in-game points.

On the other hand, there are many challenges regarding the use of cryptocurrencies within gaming environments that deserve attention. For example, [57] identified gambling as one problem in the current scenario of the eSports. The game currency and the direct connection between players/athletes and the spectators' interference can generate ethical issues about adjustment of results, corruption and economic manipulation. Those aspects deserve attention and future studies about the impact of game currencies in the actual scene of eSports. In fact, connecting cryptocurrencies and traditional sports could become a new tendency beyond the eSports, perhaps achieving the conventional sports marketing management models.

The potential for exploration of the boundaries between gaming and currencies is huge, and it requires more investigation for further and stronger conclusions. Trends like VR and AR games like *Pokemon Go* could generate an extensive competition not just for points but for using cryptocurrencies. Mobile gamers might be able to compete and collaborate in other levels, using geo-localisation strategies, for example. In VR environments, other types of economies might be explored. Players could exchange experiences and not just virtual goods, sharing their own recording of a concert in a high immersive environment or interacting with people around the world. The opportunities are huge and a large number of new game currencies emerge daily. Thus, although there is no recipe for the use of cryptocurrencies in gaming environments, there is a large scope that should be discussed by scholars and practitioners. It is possible that in the future, we may see a new ludic economy, supported by many gaming currencies created by players and stakeholders.

## Author details

Leonardo José Mataruna-dos-Santos[1,2]* and Vanissa Wanick[3]

*Address all correspondence to: leonardo.mataruna@aue.ae

1 American University in the Emirates, Dubai, UAE

2 Coventry University—CTPSR, UK

3 University of Southampton, Southampton, UK

## References

[1] Statista. Revenue of the global eSports market 2012-2021 [Internet]; 2018. Available from: https://www.statista.com/statistics/490522/global-esports-market-revenue/. [Accessed: 2018-04-05]

[2] Newzoo. Mobile Revenues Account for More Than 50% of the Global Games Market as It Reaches $137.9 Billion in 2018 [Internet]; 2018. Available from: https://newzoo.com/insights/articles/global-games-market-reaches-137-9-billion-in-2018-mobile-games-take-half/. [Accessed: 2018-05-20]

[3] Kumar V. Making freemium work. Harvard Business Review. 2014;**92**(5):27-29

[4] Maxim J. 23 Incredible Facts and Figures about Clash of Clans [Internet]; 2015. Available from: https://www.openxcell.com/23-incredible-facts-and-figures-about-clash-of-clans. [Accessed: 2018-05-09]

[5] Business Insider. The top-grossing iPhone app makes a whopping $1.5 million a day [Internet]; 2015. Available from: http://www.businessinsider.com/clash-of-clans-earns-15-million-a-day-as-top-grossing-app-2015-6?IR=T [Accessed: 2018-04-22]

[6] Einav L, Farronato C, Levin J, Sundaresan N. Auctions versus posted prices in online markets. Journal of Political Economy. February 2018;**126**(1):178-215

[7] Lehdonvirta V. Virtual Economics: Applying Economics to the Study of Game Worlds. Proceedings of the 2005 Conference on Future Play (Future Play 2005), Lansing, MI, October 13-15, 2005. Available from SSRN: https://ssrn.com/abstract=1630302. [Accessed: 2018-06-01]

[8] Delgado-Segura S, Tanas C, Herrera-Joancomartí J. Reputation and reward: Two sides of the same Bitcoin. Sensors (Basel). 2016 May 27;**16**(6) pii: E776

[9] Marczewski A. Chapter User Types. In: Even Ninja Monkeys like to Play: Gamification, Game Thinking and Motivational Design. North Charleston, SC, USA: CreateSpace Independent Publishing Platform; 2015. pp. 65-80

[10] Wimbush S. Cryptocurrency mining is neither wasteful nor uneconomic. Nature. 2018 Mar 22;**555**(7697):443

[11] Narayanan A, Bonneau J, Felten E, Miller A, Goldfeder S. Bitcoin and Cryptocurrency Technologies: A Comprehensive Introduction. Princeton University Press; 2006

[12] Yli-Huumo J, Ko D, Choi S, Park S, Smolander K. Where is current research on Blockchain technology? A systematic review. PLoS One. 2016 Oct 3;**11**(10):e0163477

[13] Wang S, Vergne JP. Correction: Buzz factor or innovation potential: What explains Cryptocurrencies' returns? PLoS One. 2017;**12**(5):e0177659

[14] Selgin G. Synthetic commodity money. Journal of Financial Stability. 2015;**17**:92-99

[15] Phillips RC, Gorse D. Cryptocurrency price drivers: Wavelet coherence analysis revisited. PLoS One. 2018 Apr 18;**13**(4):e0195200

[16] McGinn D, Birch D, Akroyd D, Molina-Solana M, Guo Y, Knottenbelt WJ. Visualizing dynamic Bitcoin transaction patterns. Big Data. 2016 Jun;**4**(2):109-119. DOI: 10.1089/big.2015.0056

[17] Crypto Briefing. The Gamification Of Money: Crypto's Millennial Appeal | Crypto Briefing [Internet]. Available from: https://cryptobriefing.com/gamification-of-money-cryptos-millennial-appeal/ [Accessed: 2018-04-22]

[18] Giddings S. and Harvey, A. Ludic Economics 101: Introduction to Special Issue Ludic Economies. Games and Culture; 2018

[19] Maia DAS. Is Freemium a Good Revenue Model for Mobas? Analysis of Success Factors [Thesis]. Lisbon: ISCTE Business School; 2015

[20] Black J, Hashimzade N, Myles G. A Dictionary of Economics. 3rd ed. Oxford: Oxford University Press; 2009

[21] Curtis EC, Nelson S, Engel F. Literature Review in Capitalization. Boston: Grantmarkers in the Arts; 2010

[22] Murphy T. The First Level of Super Mario Bros. is Easy with Lexicographic Orderings and Time Travel...after that it gets a little tricky [Internet]; 2015. Available from: https://www.cs.cmu.edu/~tom7/mario/mario.pdf. [Accessed: 2018-07-12]

[23] Hamari J, Keronen L. Why do people play games? A meta-analysis. International Journal of Information Management. 2017;**37**(3):125-141

[24] Hamari J. Why do people buy virtual goods? Attitude toward virtual good purchases versus game enjoyment. International Journal of Information Management. 2015; **35**(3):299-308

[25] Fandom. Money cheats [Internet]; 2018. Available from: http://sims.wikia.com/wiki/Money_cheats. [Accessed: 2018-06-10]

[26] EASPORTS. FIFA Mobile [Internet]; 2018. Available from: https://www.easports.com/uk/fifa/fifa-mobile. [Accessed: 2018-06-05]

[27] Flanagan M, Nissanbaum H. Values at play in digital games. MIT Press; 2014

[28] Hartmann T. Best Gaming Cryptocurrencies. Available from: https://captainaltcoin.com/best-gaming-cryptocurrencies. [Accessed: 2018-02-27]

[29] Salman A, Razzaq MGA. Bitcoin and the world of digital currencies. In: Gokten S, editor. Financial Management from an Emerging Market Perspective. Chapter 15. London: IntechOpen; 2018. DOI: 10.5772/intechopen.71294

[30] Coinmarketcap. Global chart [Internet]; 2018. Available from: https://coinmarketcap.com/charts/. [Accessed: 2018-03-27]

[31] Alexander R. HunterCoin: The Massive Multiplayer Online Cryptocoin Game (MMOCG) [Internet]; 2014. Available from: https://bitcoinmagazine.com/articles/huntercoin-the-massive-multiplayer-online-cryptocoin-game-mmocg-1409336751/ [Accessed: 2018-06-19]

[32] Huffman, Z. Top 5 Video Game Cryptocurrency Projects [Internet]; 2018. Available from: https://nulltx.com/top-5-video-game-cryptocurrency-projects [Accessed: 2018-03-27]

[33] Stanley A. Blockchain Game Momentum Builds with EON Foundation $5M Seed Round [Internet]; 2018. Available from: https://www.forbes.com/sites/astanley/2018/06/07/blockchain-game-momentum-builds-with-eon-foundation-5m-seed-round/#2276337934b0 [Accessed: 2018-06-07]

[34] Kariuki D. Top Game-based Cryptocurrencies and Tokens [Internet]; 2018. Available from: https://www.cryptomorrow.com/2018/01/08/game-based-cryptocurrencies. [Accessed: 2018-02-17]

[35] Wanick V, Mataruna-Dos-Santos LJ, Guimarães-Mataruna AF. The role of video-games in mega-events: footprints connections. In: Mataruna-Dos-Santos LJ, Pena BG, editors. Mega Events Footprints: Past, Present and Future. Available from: https://matarunadotorg.files.wordpress.com/2017/09/2017_e-book_footprints_ book_download.pdf. Rio de Janeiro: Engenho; 2017, 2017. pp. 301-319. ISBN: 978-85-69153-02-3 [Accessed: 2018-04-23]

[36] Filchenko, M. A Comparison between Esports and Traditional Sports ART 108: Introduction to Games Studies; 2018

[37] Guimarães-Mataruna AF, Wanick V, Range D. Mataruna-dos-Santos, L.J. Rio de Janeiro e-games showcase 2016: Where are the olympic values? In: Todt N et al., editors. Fórum de Estudos Olímpicos 2017: Estudos e Pesquisas. Rio de Janeiro: Universidade Santa Ursula; 2017, 2017. p. 42

[38] Graham BA. eSports to be a medal event at 2022 Asian Games [Internet]; 2017. Available from: https://www.theguardian.com/sport/2017/apr/18/esports-to-be-medal-sport-at-2022-asian-games. [Accessed: 2018-05-25]

[39] Buijsman M. Console Esports Viewership Is on the Rise, Driven by Call of Duty and FIFA [Internet]; 2018. Available from: https://newzoo.com/insights/articles/console-esports-viewership-is-on-the-rise/. [Accessed: 2018-05-04]

[40] EGBA. European Gaming and Betting Association. Sports betting: commercial and integrity issues [Internet]; 2018. Available from: http://www.egba.eu/media/Sports-Betting-Report-FINAL.pdf. [Accessed: 2018-04-02]

[41] Mataruna-Dos-Santos LJ, Pena BG. Mega Events Footprints. Rio de Janeiro: Engenho; 2017

[42] Kahle LR, Close AG. Consumer Behaviour Knowledge for Effective Sports and Event Marketing. London: Routledge; 2011

[43] Funk DC. Consumer Behaviour in Sport and Events. Burlington: Elsevier; 2008

[44] Nagle TT, Müller G. The Strategy and Tactics of Pricing: A Guide to Growing more Profitably. 6th ed. Oxon: Routledge; 2018

[45] Ouliaris S. What are economic models? Finance & Development. 2011, June;**48**(2)

[46] Järvinen A. Understanding video games as emotional experiences. In: Perron B, Wolf MJ, editors. The Video Game Theory Reader 2. Oxon: Routledge; 2009. pp. 85-108

[47] Buckley KE, Anderson CA. A Theoretical Model of the Effects and Consequences of Playing Video Games. In: Vorderer P, Bryant J, editors. Playing Video Games: Motives, Responses, and Consequences. Mahwah, NJ: LEA; 2006. pp. 363-378

[48] Perron B, Wolf MJ. The Video Game Theory Reader 2. Oxon: Routledge; 2009

[49] Wann DL, Schrader MP. Team identification and the enjoyment of watching a sporting event. Perceptual and Motor Skills. 1997;**84**(3):954-954

[50] Microsoft. Mixer: the next generation of live game streaming [Internet]; 2018. Available from: https://www.xbox.com/en-US/mixer. [Accessed: 2018-05-07]

[51] Lokhman N, Karashchuk O, Kornilova O. Analysis of eSports as a commercial activity. Business Perspectives, Problems and Perspective Management. 2018;**16**(1):207-213

[52] Caru. Pokemon Go [Internet]; 2018. Available from: https://www.pokemongo.com. [Accessed: 2018-05-25]

[53] Pardes A. IKEA's New App Flaunts What you'll Love Most about AR [Internet]; 2017. Available from: https://www.wired.com/story/ikea-place-ar-kit-augmented-reality. [Accessed: 2018-05-11]

[54] Rockstar Games. Thriving Economy & Commerce [Internet] 2018. Available from: https://www.rockstargames.com/V/lsbc/thriving-economy. [Accessed: 2018-06-18]

[55] Griffiths MD. Is the buying of loot boxes in video games a form of gambling or gaming? Gaming Law Review. 2018;**22**(1):52-54

[56] IGN. Stock Market. Available from: https://www.ign.com/wikis/gta-5/Stock_Market [Internet]; 2018. [Accessed: 2018-07-03]

[57] Bányai F, Griffiths MD, Király O, Demetrovics Z. The Psychology of Esports: A Systematic Literature Review. 2018:1-15

Section 4

# Cryptocurrency Exchanges

Chapter 5

# On the Origin of the Value of Cryptocurrencies

Er'el Granot

Additional information is available at the end of the chapter

http://dx.doi.org/10.5772/intechopen.79451

**Abstract**

Bitcoin and other cryptocurrencies received a lot of criticism during the last 9 years. It is not surprising that this criticism came from organizations that are threatened by the crypto revolution (banks, government, central banks, finance companies, etc.). Nevertheless, it is very surprising to hear criticism from economics schools, which oppose central banking and advocate free choice in currencies (such as the Austrian school of economics). Unlike the ordinary criticism (that Bitcoin is a scam, a bubble, etc.), which can easily be refuted, the criticism of part of the Austrian school economists is based on interesting arguments, which requires a different level of explanation. For example, it was claimed that Bitcoin should be worthless; otherwise, it contradicts Mises' regression theorem. The object of the chapter is twofold: first to explain why the criticism is unfounded and second to analyze the origin of the value of Bitcoin and other cryptocoins from the perspective of the Austrian school of economics. In particular, it is explained that Bitcoin does not contradict the regression theorem for two reasons. First, the initial value estimation can be a random event, and second, the Bitcoin network (even now) has a nonmonetary value.

**Keywords:** cryptocurrencies, Bitcoin, blockchain, regression theorem, Mises, Austrian school of economics, the value of money

## 1. Introduction

Bitcoin is based on three technologies: the Internet, encryption methods, and the new blockchain technology. Unlike these technologies, the Bitcoin revolution was both a technological revolution and a monetary one. It completely changed the monetary world, and it seems that its invention opened a Pandora box, whose effect cannot be underestimated or predicted. Since its inception in 2009, the Bitcoin project had many opponents, and like any successful project, their number increases gradually.

It is not very surprising to hear criticism from the industries and organization, which feel intimidated by the new invention. One would expect to find criticism from leaders in the banking industries, the insurance, and investment industries and, of course, from politicians. It is not even surprising to find criticism in the academic world, since, after all, one of the main tasks of the academic world is to instill past knowledge into the future generation and to be skeptical of new ideas.

On the other hand, since Bitcoin is a decentralized technology, it was warmly adopted by anarchist organizations worldwide [1–3], but for similar reasons, it was attacked by many others [4–9]. Some attacked the Bitcoin from the fear of shaking the current centers of powers, but most attacked it out of ignorance. Strangely enough, even in the libertarian community, which in general embraced the new currency, there are some that used allegedly Austrian economics arguments to debunk the foundation of the Bitcoin economy [10–14].

In general, we encounter two strategies to attack Bitcoin: (1) presenting multiple minor or even clearly erroneous arguments. Consequently, the arguments keep reappearing, despite the fact that they are constantly refuted. And (2) using fundamental economic laws to allegedly demonstrate that Bitcoin does not possess the essential properties of money.

The object of the chapter is twofold: (1) to present and refute all the main arguments in a single chapter and (2) to utilize these arguments to reinvestigate the origin of the source of money in general and cryptocurrency in particular.

So, let us begin with the simple arguments:

## 2. Is Bitcoin a Ponzi scheme?

The most common criticism against Bitcoin is that Bitcoin is actually a Ponzi scheme [7, 10]. Clearly, there is no resemblance between the two. A Ponzi scheme is a fraudulent investment operation. The investors are made to believe that they gain from the investment operation, while in fact, the money comes from new investment, that is, a Ponzi scheme is a pyramid fraud.

While some cryptocurrencies or tokens do seem to be a Ponzi scheme, Bitcoin is definitely not. Everything about Bitcoin: its algorithm, its network, and its development projects are completely transparent. The network, the mining process, and the entire project are all decentralized. There are no managers, no organizers, and no control. Therefore, there could be no fraud.

Bitcoin does not even have a pyramid structure. An investor in Bitcoin can make a profit by selling it at a higher price, just like in any other trade. Unlike pyramid structures, the owner of Bitcoins does not have to convince multiple people to invest in order to make a profit.

It is true that in both cases, the first investors gain more than the last ones, and that their profit rises with the number of traders. However, by the law of demand, it is clear that the price rises with the increase in demand, that is, the price increases with the number of buyers. This is valid for any commodity, and Bitcoin is no exception. This is definitely not a pyramid structure's fingerprint. Moreover, the whole network structure is different. A pyramid is a centralized structure, where there is a clear asymmetry between investors and all profits eventually dissipate toward the founders of the pyramid (this is a "top-down" business model). Bitcoin is a decentralized network, where all the Bitcoins' owners have the same status. Moreover, the founders of a crypto network may not even own a share in this network, or they can sell their share, if they have one (like Charlie Lee, the founder of the Litecoin network, who recently sold all his Litecoins).

## 3. Bitcoin is a bubble

Another common criticism is that Bitcoin and the other cryptocurrencies are a bubble [4, 6, 8]. This claim is not a very informative one. What does it mean? Does it mean that the Bitcoin price is too high? In a free market, the price is always right. If there is something "wrong" with the price, then it means that the market is not really free. When there is a housing bubble, it does not mean that there is something wrong with the houses, or that the sellers are greedier than they usually are, but it does mean that the government manipulates the interest rate and subsidizes bad mortgages, etc.

Therefore, any "bubble" claim is actually not a criticism against Bitcoin, but a claim against something external to its network—probably against governments. If everyone buys cryptocurrencies, it is probably because the public has no other investment channels. The banking interest is practically zero; the stock market is too high after 10 consecutive years of rising prices; and the housing market is recovering from the latest collapse. The fact that Bitcoin is in a state of a bubble, whatever that means, cannot be used as evidence to the argument that Bitcoin is worthless.

As Ludwig Wittgenstein wrote, "For whenever we test anything, we are already presupposing something that is not tested." Similarly, when one believes the price of Bitcoin is too high, he presupposes that Bitcoin has *some* value.

## 4. Bitcoin yields no return

Another repeating argument is that Bitcoin is not a real asset in the sense that it does not yield any return. Unlike stocks or real estates, which yield dividends and rents, Bitcoin does not "yield" anything. People purchase Bitcoin only to sell it later.

But this is a strange argument, since, after all, money never yields return. A one-dollar note does not yield a return. It will be worth 1$ forever. Nevertheless, people "purchase" dollars only to "sell" them later for goods. This is exactly the function of money and the same applies to Bitcoin.

## 5. The Bitcoin's volatility

One very common attack on Bitcoin is that it must be useless as money (or currency) since it has very high volatility [12, 13].

Clearly, if an asset's value is very volatile, then it is less likely to be adopted as a unit of account, which is one of the properties of money. However, it should not considerably affect its prospects to be used as *a medium of exchange*. Even today, most Bitcoin transactions are quantified in US dollars, that is, in these transactions, Bitcoin is used as a medium of exchange, while the US dollar is used as a unit of account. However, it should be stressed that in these transactions, the dollar takes no role. Bitcoin is currently exploring a new territory, in which it is used as a medium of exchange, but yet to be used as a unit of account (on this discrepancy see Ref. [15]).

Moreover, the usage of the volatility criterion is useful only in close-to-equilibrium's markets. In the case of Bitcoin, the price increases exponentially, which is a clear sign of a nonequilibrium scenario. Exponential rise is an indication of a constant amplification process, which cannot occur in the vicinity of equilibria. In this case, it is clear that the volatility will increase exponentially as well. Therefore, there could be two options: (A) the approximately constant amplification process is close to its end, in which case the market will converge to a semiequilibrium state, and the volatility will decrease dramatically. (B) The constant amplification process is going to last for some time, in which case the value of Bitcoin will continue to rise dramatically.

Therefore, in both cases, the attractiveness of Bitcoin will increase, and in any case, the high volatility in an exponentially growing process cannot be used as an argument for the claim that Bitcoin is worthless. It is only a sign that the crypto market is in its infancy stages.

In an exponentially growing economy, the volatility should be evaluated in logarithmic scale, and in this scale, the Bitcoins' volatility actually declines.

## 6. The hoarding dilemma

Another important claim is that Bitcoin is worthless as a medium of exchange because most people, who purchased it, hoard the coins [12, 13]. Since most people regard Bitcoin as a store of value and "Hodl" (the crypto nickname for hold) the coins, how can it be used as a medium of exchange? This claim is often heard even in the crypto community, where the holders are encouraged to exchange their coins with goods, that is, to sell and buy the coins repeatedly (e.g., Ivan Liljeqvist and Rick Falkvinge). However, the two properties of money are tightly linked. A good cannot be a store of value unless it is a medium of exchange and vice versa. How can an object be valuable, without the option of exchanging it for something else? How can something be a medium of exchange, unless it is valuable?

Moreover, hoarding takes place only when people expect that the coins' price will rise in the future. In this case, fewer coins are used in circulation and, as a consequence, their price increases. This is the mechanism that persuades the hoarders to part with their coins.

## 7. A deflationary economy

The hoarding dilemma is a very important point because it is related to another criticism: how can Bitcoin be used as a medium of exchange while being a deflationary currency? In a deflationary monetary economy, the argument continues, prices decrease perpetually, and therefore people have no incentive to buy anything, for they know that they will probably get it for less money in the future. In such an economy, consumption decreases, and the economy stagnates.

There are several problems with this argument. First, there is a problem of definition. Bitcoin is an inflationary currency, not a deflationary one since the number of coins increases gradually. It is true, however, that its rate decreases, and eventually the total number of coins is limited (around 21 million). Consequently, in a progressing economy, which is based on Bitcoin, eventually, the Bitcoin inflation will be lower than the economy's growth rate. In such an economy, the products' prices will eventually decrease. This state is wrongly termed "deflationary" [16, 17]. However, and this brings us to the second misconception, there is nothing wrong with rising prices. In fact, the economic sectors, which experience decreasing prices, are the sectors with the highest growth rate. The computer industry belongs to this category. Computer prices perpetually decline for decades, while the industry is growing. Not only that people did not stop from buying computers, but computers' sales are gradually increasing.

People have needs, and as economists explain, they have a time preference, that is, they do not like to postpone gratifications [16–18]. If they need a computer, they will eventually buy it, and decreasing prices is a good incentive to make the purchase. Eventually, they will buy the computer.

The third misconception is that saving is worse than spending and therefore people should be encouraged to spend their money. In fact, unlike the Keynesian thinking, over consumption is the enemy of economic growth. Clearly, people have to buy to encourage production; however, the economy cannot grow unless there is enough savings and investments. That is, as was explained by Hayek (in "the paradox of savings" [19]), when people save their money, they only *postpone* their consumption; they do not stop consumption altogether. Saving is a crucial ingredient in any economic growth, and therefore, there is nothing harmful in an economy with rising prices. In fact, at the end of the nineteenth century, when the American economy was based on the gold standard, the US experienced one of its best economic eras during a deflationary period [20, 21].

Evidence shows that any economy will gain from a "deflationary" currency, such as Bitcoin (or even gold, for that matter). However, if, in the future, it will be clear that there are some benefits to inflationary currency, then there are many other coins, in which inflation is part of their algorithm, for which case there is no upper limit to the number of coins. Let the market decide on the best inflationary/deflationary algorithm.

## 8. Bitcoin and the government

There is a claim that governments may create a competitive coin to Bitcoin, and simultaneously, the governments can outlaw Bitcoin. Indeed, the government can create a token of its own, and it seems that some governments seriously think about such an enterprise [22–24]. However, it is not clear what would be their motives. If these governments intend to create simply a true decentralized competitor to Bitcoin, then they would face two problems: (1) a government would never be able to compete against the decentralization level of Bitcoin and (2) with a decentralized coin, the government would lose all its benefits of controlling the national currency, that is, by replacing fiat currency with cryptocurrency, the government literally kills the goose that lays golden eggs.

If the government plans on creating a centralized coin (i.e., government-controlled currency), then it could not rely on the good reputation of decentralized coins. In this case, the government would encounter a great difficulty to sell the coin to the Bitcoin community (see what happens with the new Venezuela's Petro).

Governments can confront the problem differently, and it can try to ban Bitcoin. This is evidently possible de jure but not de facto. The more the government manipulates the currency, the more the people need cryptocurrencies (see, e.g., the case of Zimbabwe, India, and Venezuela).

## 9. Technology-based money

There is a good question regarding Bitcoin's longevity. Bitcoin, the claim argues, is a technological invention. In principle, there is no reason that it would not be defeated by competing technologies. Unlike gold, which would exist forever, Bitcoin is a technology that changes in time. This is an interesting argument; however, in fact, this argument only emphasizes the similarities between gold and Bitcoin. Gold is here to stay, but so does Bitcoin. Actually, due to its decentralization, it would be extremely difficult to eliminate the entire Bitcoin blockchain. To achieve that, every copy of the blockchain should be erased. The chances of that are extremely low. Clearly, the value of the blockchain can decline substantially, but this is equivalent to a decline in the price of gold due to a lack of (technological or financial) interest. Therefore, gold is not better money than Bitcoin due to the fact that "while Bitcoin can be overthrown by competitive technologies, gold will exist forever." In fact, they both will probably survive for a very long time, and both may lose their value due to competitive technologies, because, in its essence, gold is also a monetary technology.

Having said that, it must be emphasized that a replacement of a monetary technology is a very challenging task. Financial markets are very conservative.

Gold has no clear chemical advantage over (for example) platinum, palladium, or iridium, and the main reason that gold is preferred over these precious metals is its early adoption as a medium of exchange (possibly due to its unique yellowish color). It may be instructive to note that there have been several attempts in the history to replace gold with other metals (iron in Sparta, copper in Rome, and even silver in the US); however, these attempts did not affect the gold's hegemony worldwide.

The same thing applies to Bitcoin. Bitcoin enjoys the network effect due to its early adoption. The gold's unique color and its plasticity made it relatively resistant to counterfeiting. However, gold counterfeiting is still possible (e.g., by covering tungsten with a layer of gold, because tungsten and gold have almost the same density), while Bitcoin cannot be counterfeited.

http://dx.doi.org/10.5772/intechopen.79451

## 10. Genuine scarcity

This brings us to a well-known argument, that says that Bitcoin, like any other digital asset, is not scarce, and therefore can be repeatedly reproduced. The knowledgeable Bitcoin's opponent, which uses this argument, does not mean that the number of Bitcoins can be increased ad infinitum. He means that the algorithm can be copied and an infinite amount of rival crypto networks can be created. In fact, during the writing of these lines, there are literally thousands of cryptocurrencies networks: Bitcoins, Ethereum, Ripple, Bitcoin Cash, Cardano, Litecoin, Stellar, NEO, EOS, and IOTA to mention only the first 10 within the highest market cap list. Moreover, each one of these coins can be forked to other coins. The original Bitcoin network was forked many times to Bitcoin cash, Bitcoin gold, Bitcoin diamond, Bitcoin segwit2x, etc.

The argument is, therefore, that digital assets, like cryptocurrencies, can be even worse than fiat currencies, for while fiat currencies' inflation is regulated by central banks, and the number of cryptocurrencies can be inflated uncontrollably. However, Bitcoin is not only an algorithm. Indeed, the cost of copying the algorithm is negligible. But Bitcoin is also a very secure network. Every new Bitcoin-clone does not benefit from the same level of security. The more computational power is invested in the network; the more secure the network is, and the more people would find it safe to invest their money in it.

Bitcoin may lose its hegemony in the crypto sphere; however, as was explained above, it would be very difficult for new networks to pose a real threat to Bitcoin due to its proven high security and reliability.

## 11. Bitcoin transactions are too slow and too expensive

Recently, the Bitcoin adversaries took advantage of the heavy load on the Bitcoin network, which caused slow and high fee transactions, to claim that the Bitcoin does not deliver its promises—Bitcoin transactions are too slow and too expensive. Soon, they predict, the Bitcoin network will be so cumbersome, that transactions will become unfeasible, and the Bitcoin project will be abandoned. This is indeed a problem. But this is a technological problem and not a fundamental one. It may explain why the Bitcoin market dominance declines, but it can never be used to explain why Bitcoin should be worthless. Clearly, the Bitcoin developers are aware of these problems and work constantly to mitigate the harmful effects of the network load.

Several technological improvements have been suggested and implemented (SegWit, lighting network, atomic swap, and even raising block size in a forked versions of Bitcoin).

Moreover, there are countless other currencies, whose transactions are much quicker and cheaper, and yet their value is considerably lower than the value of the Bitcoin network. Despite the fact that the technology is yet in its infancy stages, and there are still numerous technological challenges, the value of Bitcoin keeps on growing.

Therefore, these facts should be an argument for Bitcoin and not against it, because these problems show that the need for reliable decentralized currency in the modern markets is so high, that people keep purchasing it despite the high transaction costs (and despite the fact that there are low cost but less proven alternatives).

## 12. Currencies backed by nothing

A very popular argument against cryptocurrencies is that they are backed by nothing: "They are neither backed by gold nor are they backed by governments."

Clearly, these are two different arguments. President Nixon, in 1971, was responsible to complete the monetary experiment that began at 1944 with the Bretton Woods system. Since then, there is not a single fiat currency in the entire globe, which is backed by gold or by any other commodity. Hence, a commodity backup is not a crucial ingredient in the making of money. As for the second argument, what does it mean that the currency is backed by the government?

Clearly, if the government backs its currency by forbidding the usage of other currencies (in its geographical territory), then it enforces a certain minimum value for the currency. However, not all governments can or do that. In most countries, the population can make economic transactions with many currencies. Most governments back their currencies by enforcing tax payment with them. Similarly, the governments pay their employees with the national currency. However, these conducts are equivalent to the presence of a rich man in a market, who declares that any economic transaction with him can take place only with a certain currency. As richer this man is, the higher will be the value of this currency. Clearly, a government is equivalent to a very rich man, but the differences are quantitative rather than qualitative ones.

One of the most instructive examples in this regard is the Swiss dinars in northern Iraq during the gulf war [25]. This is a very interesting example, which vividly illustrates the fact that paper money can be used as a medium of exchange, despite the fact that it is backed neither by any commodity nor by any government.

## 13. Dependence on the current monetary system

An argument against Bitcoin, which was very common in its early years, is that Bitcoin is not a real medium of exchange because most traders, which accept Bitcoin, convert them to fiat currency almost immediately after the transaction.

Nowadays, this argument is heard less since many sellers prefer Bitcoin over fiat money. They prefer spending their fiat money and receive and keep their cryptos. Moreover, nowadays many employees are paid in cryptocurrency.

However, it is important to stress that whether the users of Bitcoin prefer to make an additional transaction after selling a product, that is, to convert the crypto to fiat, is irrelevant to the validity of Bitcoin as a medium of exchange. First, there is no praxeological difference between the exchange of Bitcoin with fiat and the exchange of Bitcoin with other goods. If a seller prefers to convert Bitcoin into fiat currencies, it only means that he had decided to use Bitcoin as a medium of exchange to purchase the fiat currencies. Moreover, one should not ignore the fact that the main reason that sellers prefer to convert their cryptos back into fiat is due to government regulations (mainly taxation) and has nothing to do with the fundamental monetary properties of Bitcoin.

## 14. Bitcoin and economic calculations

Some Austrian economists used the volatility problem and the last argument to claim that Bitcoin cannot be used for economic calculations. Since economic calculations are essential to any modern economy [16], it is futile, according to them, to replace the current fiat currency with Bitcoin. However, economic calculations can be made with any commodity. When a businessman has four bottles of wines, and he needs to choose between two production alternatives: one alternative that will eventually yield three additional bottles and a second one that will eventually yield five bottles, he will choose the latter. The same thing applies to Bitcoin. Crypto traders already practice this kind of economic calculations using Bitcoin.

However, volatility is indeed a problem (mainly in intra-temporal calculations, i.e., interest rates), which prevents wide adoption. Nevertheless, as was explained above, the volatility gradually declines, and it is one of the infancy problems of Bitcoin, and it is not a fundamental one.

## 15. Bitcoin and the division of labor

Division of labor cannot exist in a nonmonetary economy. The presence of money drives people to specialize and increases their productivity beyond their personal needs. They can trade the surplus of their production in order to pursue higher gratifications (for the analysis of production in the presence of specialization, see Ref. [26]).

Therefore, any adoption of Bitcoin as a medium of exchange should be accompanied by an upgrade of the division of labor. Is there any evidence for this?

The problem is that it is almost impossible to attribute scientifically a specific improvement in the division of labor to a specific cause. However, it is clear that if a person prefers using Bitcoin than other currency, then he must have found it useful and more efficient for him. Therefore, this individual can spend the surplus time in further specialization.

Consequently, in a free market, any unregulated usage of Bitcoin (or anything else for that matter) is a circumstantial evidence for upgrading the division of labor.

## 16. Bitcoin and property rights

Property rights are subtle issues. There is a fundamental claim that intangible objects, like digital assets or ideas, cannot be owned. The claim is based on the presumption that property rights and private ownership are essential to manage scarce resources in the real world. Thus, according to this view, only scarce resources (like, land, houses, gold, etc.) can be owned, while resources that are not scarce (like, ideas, patents, text, digital pictures, etc.) and that can be easily reproduced cannot be owned [27]. Bitcoin is a chimera, in that regard, since it is both digital, that is, intangible, and scarce. In fact, the essence of the blockchain technology is the creation of scarce digital assets. That is, the blockchain creates artificial scarcity.

Therefore, despite the complex philosophical issue, I believe there is a consensus that Bitcoins can be owned, and property rights can and should be applied to it.

There is a claim, however, that Bitcoin advocates ignore traditional property rights, contracts, and traditional legal systems, which were developed and refined for millennia [12].

It is true that currently, it is easier to evade law enforcement using cryptocurrencies than using most bank transactions. The facts that there is nothing tangible in the Bitcoin network and that digital transactions can take place without the regulated banking system complicate law enforcement. However, on the one hand, it can be regarded as a technical difficulty, which may be solved using artificial intelligence technologies, and on the other hand, one may argue that these properties of the Bitcoin network only strengthen property rights, because they prevent government confiscation of private property (private money).

Not only aren't crypto networks against contracts, but also smart contracts are an integral part of these networks. The most well-known is the Ethereum network, but there are many more cryptocurrencies with this property (like Neo, EOS, Cardano, etc.), and even the Bitcoin network can support smart contracts (Mastercoin, Rootstock, Particl, etc.).

Therefore, the blockchain technology eliminates the need for (external) law enforcement in some cases, because the contracts are enforced within the blockchain itself.

In general, cryptocurrencies strengthen private property and property rights. They do not weaken them.

## 17. Bitcoin and crime

Some politicians and economists believe that Bitcoin and other cryptocurrencies have no value to society since most of their users are outlaws and criminals [28].

For one thing, one has to make a distinction between the different cryptocurrencies. Most of the criminal activity was transferred from the Bitcoin network to the more private cryptos (such as Monero, Zcash, Verge, etc.) since transactions in the Bitcoin network can be traced.

Moreover, most of the illegal trade that takes place on the Internet belongs to the category of victimless crimes (like drugs, gambling, and tax evasion), whose prohibition is disputed.

In any case, the illegal activities that take place on the network only emphasize the fact that the crypto networks are valuable for at least some of the people, and in a market economy, when a commodity is valuable for some of the people, then it is valuable to the entire economy.

## 18. Bitcoin and egalitarianism

There is a claim that a Bitcoin-based economy would increase wealth inequality. This argument is based on the fact that most of the Bitcoin wealth is concentrated in a minuscule amount of Bitcoin addresses [29]. But clearly, wallets and addresses are not persons. Almost every user holds several wallets, and a wallet can and does generate multiple addresses mainly for privacy reasons.

This argument suffers from an additional fallacy: the distribution of money in a population does not determine the distribution of wealth. Quite the contrary, the distribution of wealth determines the distribution of money. In a free economy, people are paid for creating wealth. Since Bitcoin economy has a higher resemblance to a free economy than our current fiat economy, it seems that in a Bitcoin-based economy, the money distribution will be fairer than the current one.

## 19. The value of Bitcoin

There is a claim that Bitcoin is worthless, because it answers no real need and solves no real problem. This claim can easily be refuted.

Bitcoin is a global, decentralized, highly liquid, and pseudo-anonymous asset. Therefore, in any transaction, which requires all these properties, the benefits of using Bitcoin over other currencies are clear. Moreover, that is exactly the reason that most people do not appreciate these properties. First, most people are unaware of the damage caused by centralized monetary systems. Second, only rarely do they perform international financial transactions in large volumes. Third, most people are against anonymous transactions.

However, the benefits of Bitcoin are widely recognized in the following cases:

(1) Where the centralized monetary system completely collapses (e.g., Venezuela and Zimbabwe). (2) Where the government confiscates its own citizen's assets (e.g., Cyprus and Saudi Arabia). (3) Among populations, which are excluded from the financial and banking systems (e.g., bankrupted citizens and minors). (4) Among outcasted populations (e.g., drug users and gamblers). (5) Among people who are keener on their privacy (e.g., tax evaders and porn users). (6) Among frequent travelers/flyers.

In general, it is clear that the Bitcoin technology has a clear value wherever censorship-resistance is required. Money is one example, social media is another (e.g., Steem, LBRY, Memo).

As was mentioned above, in a market economy, when an asset is valuable to some people, then it is valuable to the entire economy. Consequently, people who do not belong to any of these populations can still regard Bitcoin as a safe haven for their money.

However, the fact that Bitcoin is valuable only increases the mystery as for the *origin* of its value. In the previous sections, we have presented the problems in arguments, which claim that Bitcoin should be worthless. Before we present the last argument, which will lead us to the *origin* of the Bitcoin's value, it is instructive to discuss incorrect explanations, from which we will learn what *cannot* explain the origin of the value of Bitcoin.

## 20. Backed by energy

It is repeatedly mentioned by crypto advocates that Bitcoin is backed by proof-of-work, or, that it is backed by energy or by the mining's electricity.

In particular, such an explanation was used by John McAfee to justify his prediction of the Bitcoin price at the end of 2020 [30]. The argument goes like that: currently, it costs several million dollars to mine 1800 BTC (the current daily yield). Within few decades, the mining rate will decrease substantially, while there is no reason to assume that the cost will decline (more plausible that it will rise). Therefore, one may conclude that because Bitcoin's mining cost will rise, its price must rise as well.

This is a very common error that is based on the classical economists' theory of value—the labor theory of value. This theory, which was developed by Smith, Ricardo and their followers (including Marx), was based on the premises that the labor is the source of value. This theory helped them to explain the water-diamond paradox, namely, why the value of diamonds is higher than the value of water, while clearly water is much more useful than diamonds. The classical economists would reply that it costs more to mine and to shape diamonds than to pump water from a nearby well. The subjectivist schools of economics, in general, and the Austrian school, in particular, would strongly disagree. Bohm-Bawerk, the well-known economist, would argue that it may be very costly to prepare a mud pie, nevertheless, the mud pie is still worthless. The Austrian economists would argue that the classical economists made it all wrong. It is the price of the product that determines its cost and not the vice-versa. That is, if a producer evaluates that he can sell a product for 1000$, he will be willing to pay production costs, which are lower than 1000$. Clearly, the competition enforces the producer to lower the product's price until it is close to the product's cost. However, had he not known that he could sell the product at a price higher than the cost he would not have produced it.

The same thing applies to any product, and mining is not an exception. As long as the market price of gold is higher than the cost of mining, then mining will continue, otherwise, the miners would stop the mining process. That is, the market cost of gold (approximately 1200$/ounce today) determines the maximum cost of mining. In the case of Bitcoin, the mining process cannot stop. In fact, since every 10 min a new block is added to the blockchain, then the algorithm keeps adjusting the mining difficulty to maintain a constant rate of block production. Therefore, the algorithm makes sure that the mining cost would remain below the market price so that mining would never stop.

## 21. Too costly to mine

A similar reasoning appears in a different argument against Bitcoin: the Bitcoin mining costs are extremely high, and even now, its electricity consumption is equal to that of a small country (like Ireland). Within several years, the costs would be gigantic, and it would be unprofitable to mine additional coins.

Again, this is a complete misunderstanding of the mining process. As was explained above, unlike gold mining, there is no given external cost for mining Bitcoin. The causality between cost and prices works in the opposite direction—Bitcoin prices determine the cost of mining. Therefore, at any given time, the users of the Bitcoin network are the ones who determine the amount of money they are willing to invest in the network security. That is, first, the mining cost cannot increase beyond the amount the users are willing to pay, and second, the electricity cost is not a wasted investment; it is a measure of the network security. The more people trust the Bitcoin network, the more they are willing to invest in it. Consequently, the Bitcoin price increases, and so does, as a byproduct, the mining cost, which measures the network computation power. That is, the more secure the network is, the more trustworthy it becomes in practice via the price mechanism. This is a positive feedback, which strengthens the network. However, there is a limit to the cost of security, which people are willing to pay in any financial transaction. This limit determines the mining cost.

It is interesting that a similar argument was put against the gold standard. Followers of the monetary school of economics argued that unlike fiat money, gold mining is a waste of useful resources, which can be directed to other useful industrial sectors. The answer of the Austrian school was that it is a small price to pay to prevent the government from inflating the amount of money [31]. The Austrian economists have a nice analogy: why so many resources are invested in steel locks? Wouldn't it be smarter had we replaced them with paper locks and allocate the steel to better uses? This is clearly a rhetorical question. Security is a costly business. We pay for security and safety.

This is an important point. In a stationary economy, or, in the Austrian school terminology, the Evenly Rotating Economy (ERE), the future is already known, and there are neither surprises nor risks. Consequently, there is no need for money. In the ERE, money has no function. People need money only in states of uncertainty. Money helps relieve the sense of uncertainty. However, counterfeiting is a source of concern. Fiat money is susceptible to the whims of the government. Governments can (and do) inflate the money supply indefinitely.

The supply of gold, on the other hand, is regulated by the market, since gold counterfeiting is extremely difficult. Only when the market price exceeds the mining cost, new gold is generated by mining.

The same reasoning applies to Bitcoin. However, there are some very important differences: as was explained above, it is more difficult to counterfeit Bitcoin than gold, let alone fiat currency. Moreover, the ability to counterfeit fiat currency and gold is independent of their value. Therefore, as their value rises, additional counterfeiting attempts are made.

The opposite is true for Bitcoin. The difficulty to attack the Bitcoin network is proportional to the Hash power of the Bitcoin mining; however, the cost of this power is proportional to the price of Bitcoin (since most of the Bitcoins have already been mined). Therefore, unlike fiat money and unlike gold, as the price of Bitcoin rises, it becomes more difficult to attack the network (Bitcoin's equivalent of counterfeiting).

To summarize this point, the high mining cost is not a waste—it is a security investment.

## 22. Scarcity and value

Another misconception about the origin of the value of Bitcoin is that unlike fiat money, which is created "out of thin air," the number of Bitcoins is fixed and cannot be changed, and this inherent scarcity is the source of its value.

First, as was explained above, Bitcoin is also inflationary. In fact, the important characteristic of the decentralized crypto coins is not that coins cannot be created "out of thin air," but that their creation is fully determined by the well-known protocol and cannot be manipulated by a central entity (i.e., governments). Therefore, the users can take account of the inflation parameters into their future financial contracts. This property of cryptocurrencies is a clear advantage they have over fiat currencies. In fact, this is a major advantage even over commodities backed currencies, such as gold, since the future mining rate of gold is unknown, while cryptocurrencies are created in a predetermined manner.

Second, scarcity, by itself, cannot be the source of value. Using Bohm-Bawerk example, the fact that a certain mud pie cannot be reproduced is, in itself, an insufficient demand to make it valuable. Scarcity is a necessary but insufficient condition for value creation.

## 23. The regression theorem and the *origin* of value

It was Karl Helfferich who formulated in 1903 the vicious circle of money [32]. The marginal value theory of Menger, the forefather of the Austrians school, can explain why a handful of diamond worth considerably more than the buckets of water, despite the fact that water is clearly more essential to human existence than diamonds are [33]; however, it could not explain why a seemingly worthless object like pieces of papers can have a high value. In other words, it cannot explain why people would be willing to exchange them with commodities, which have a clear intrinsic value. It was clear that if people, for some reason, attribute value to money, then it would be a logical behavior for the individual to attribute value for money, even if he does not find it useful to himself. However, how did money gain its value in the first place, or, in others word, it is a vicious circle to say that people want money simply because people want money [32].

Mises, apparently, solved this conundrum. He said that people want money today because they anticipate that other people would want it tomorrow since they wanted it yesterday, that is, money has value today because it has value yesterday. By introducing time schedule into the description of the process, Mises circumvented the vicious circle. But he did it with a cost. This logic leads to the unavoidable conclusion that any money had, prior to its use as a medium of exchange, an intrinsic value [34].

Thus, there is an argument that Bitcoin cannot be money since it never had an intrinsic value, that is, while the US fiat dollar is valuable today since it was based on the original value of the gold dollar, which was based for millennia on the currency value of gold, which was based somewhere in the past on the commodity value of gold, they claim that Bitcoin does not have such a chain of events. One cannot find any intrinsic value in the Bitcoin genesis. While gold

http://dx.doi.org/10.5772/intechopen.79451

has an extensive commodity use in its premonetary era, Bitcoin, according to them, had no nonmonetary history and therefore cannot evolve into money.

This claim has several flaws. First, they turn Mises' argument on its head—Mises used his argument to explain how apparently worthless object can be used as a medium of exchange. Bitcoin is already a medium of exchange, which means that there are only two options, either Mises argument is erroneous or that they are missing something about Bitcoin. In fact, *Mises was not entirely accurate and Bitcoin does have a nonmonetary value*.

I would like to harness a physical analogy to explain this point—the laser.

When a laser is connected to a power supply, it emits coherent light almost instantaneously. Nowadays, lasers are very common and there is nothing special about this; however, a laser is not a light bulb, the origin of light in a laser can be regarded as a similar mystery. A laser consists of two basic elements: a light amplifier and a resonator, which is actually a feedback mechanism. Hence, a laser is a giant amplifying machine. Using the feedback, the laser keeps on amplifying the light. But wait! Where did the light originally come from? The laser has no element that generates the "original" light (i.e., the primordial photons), it only amplifies it. So where did the light originally come from? Well, actually, this is quite a mystery that nobody really knows. The source can be thermal noise, scattered light, or maybe the zero point energy. While academically it may be an interesting question, it is practically irrelevant to the laser operation. Moreover, it teaches us an important lesson—in the presence of a highly efficient amplifying process, the increase is exponential, and therefore the initial trigger is practically irrelevant. It doesn't matter whether the process started from a single photon, ten photons or a hundred, the changes in the time till it reaches equilibrium (the time, in which it grows exponentially) is negligible.

The same goes for Bitcoin. It was proven to be a rapidly accelerating phenomenon. In fact, just like the laser intensity or any other phenomenon with an approximately constant rate increase, the value of Bitcoin grew exponentially: within about 4 years it increased by a factor of a million! The technology was proven so successful that the initial value, people attributed to Bitcoin, is unimportant.

The legendary pizza transaction, which allegedly determined its initial market value (in which a couple of pizzas were sold for 10,000 BTC), could be totally different. It could have been sold for 1000 or 100,000 BTCs, and the final outcome would be almost the same and it would be determined by the equilibrium value. In fact, the entire process can start from a whim of a handful of strange geeks (see, for example [35]). That is totally sufficient, exactly like the amplifying process in a laser, which can start, for all we know, from a single photon, which accidentally was present in the laser's cavity.

In the previous paragraphs, it was explained why one does not have to prove that Bitcoin currently has an intrinsic use value in order to show that its exchange value, that is, its value as a medium of exchange, does not contradict Mises' regression theorem; nevertheless, *Bitcoin had and still has an intrinsic use value*.

Clearly, even prior to the Pizza transaction, the initial miner group attributed value to Bitcoin since they spent their time and the energy consumption of their computers to generate these Bitcoins.

Bitcoin is not the only thing that can be sent via the blockchain, in fact, almost any kind of information can be sent via the transactions, and this is an irreversible process, since any such information will remain in the blockchain for eternity, and everyone in the network will have an access to this information. Bitcoins are the cost of perpetuating the information. In other words, Bitcoins can be regarded as the "real estate" of the blockchain. The more Bitcoins a person has, the more information he can send on the blockchain. There are all kinds of data encapsulated on the blockchain: poems, prays, political statements, commercials, and even photos [36]. In fact, it is amazing how many kinds of information can be found there. It is not difficult to find many applications for this kind of information retention.

One of the special applications is the announcement of contracts. Such contracts will be confirmed by the blockchain. Or another important application is a decentralized registrar of real estate (or any other type of property). With the Bitcoin network, one can announce ownership of objects, the information will be available instantaneously, and since it is not centralized, then there is no fear of losing this information.

The important thing is to realize that there is no direct connection between this information and the value of Bitcoin. The relation is indirect. The value of these announcements is directly related to the number of nodes in the network. The more people are connected to the Bitcoin network, the more valuable this information is. Therefore, if the network is large enough, then people will like to use it by sending and announcing information. However, it is clear that when the network grows, sending information becomes more valuable, and therefore the value of the network's coin, which controls it, increases as well. The more coins a person owns, the more he controls the network. Again we see that owning Bitcoin is like owning real estate on the blockchain.

Clearly, at its inception, when the Bitcoin network was small, the value of publishing data over it was low, but then the Bitcoin's value was accordingly small. In fact, in its genesis, the Bitcoin's value could have been only the subjective value of the first few geeks, who mined it (including Satoshi himself). When the network grows, the Bitcoin value increases exponentially, just like the laser power.

Nowadays, the fees of sending information over the blockchain are quite high, and therefore people seldom use the blockchain for broadcasting information. As a consequence, they tend to forget that the Bitcoin network has a clear nonmonetary use, and therefore it has a subjective use value. In any case, the fact that Bitcoin has a nonzero value does not and cannot contradict Mises' regression theorem.

## 24. Conclusions

Bitcoin has many enemies, and, as a consequence, there are many arguments, which allegedly explains, why Bitcoin should be worthless or should be banned. The truth is that Bitcoin is extremely valuable and is here to stay because it cannot be banned. On the other hand, Bitcoin has many advocates, which use inaccurate arguments to justify the origin of its value.

The fact that these arguments were presented by renowned economists shows us that our understanding about the origin of money did not change much during the last century. The mysterious Satoshi Nakamoto gave us the opportunity to revive these century-old conundrums.

The main conclusions are:

- Bitcoin is not a scheme; it is a great monetary invention, which has a clear economic value.
- It cannot and should not be banned by governments. In fact, any government's manipulation and regulation emphasize and increase the need for cryptocurrencies.
- Criminals are not the only ones who see the benefits in using cryptocurrencies. In the third world (e.g., Venezuela and Zimbabwe), cryptos are lifesavers. In general, cryptos are extremely valuable wherever censorship resistance is required, and in a global market economy, that fact creates value for everyone.
- Bitcoin does suffer from infancy problems (high volatility and high transaction costs); however, these issues are not fundamental and will be resolved eventually (we already see many signs for that). The fact that the crypto market exceeded 800B$, despite these issues, only emphasizes the need of the markets in them.
- The energy which is spent in crypto mining is not a wasted energy. It is the source of the network's security which increases the trust in the system, and in a market economy trust is a very valuable commodity.
- The easiness in the creation of new coins is not equivalent to fiat money inflation. Fiat inflation is a counterfeiting process, while the creation of new cryptos is equivalent to the creation of a new invention, which may be better, but it has to surmount the former coins' network effect.
- Bitcoin does not contradict any economical law. In particular, it does not contradict Mises' regression theorem for two grounds: first, Bitcoin was valuable for the first miners even before it was used as a medium of exchange, and the regression process can be kindled by any subjective whim; second, even now Bitcoin has a nonmonetary value (just like gold) as a "real-estate" on the Bitcoin network.

## Author details

Er'el Granot

Address all correspondence to: erel@ariel.ac.il

Department of Electrical and Electronics Engineering, Ariel University, Ariel, Israel

## References

[1] Kharpal A. WikiLeaks Founder Assange Claims he Made 50,000% Return on Bitcoin Thanks to the US Government. CNBC. October 16, 2017. Available from: https://www.cnbc.com/2017/10/16/wikileaks-julian-assange-bitcoin-50000-percent-return-thanks-to-us-government.html

[2] Lujan S. Bitcoin was Built to Incite Peaceful Anarchy. Bitcoin.com. January 9, 2016. Available from: https://news.bitcoin.com/bitcoin-built-incite-peaceful-anarchy/

[3] del Castillo M. Guns & Crypto: How Bitcoin is Helping Keep Cody Wilson's Anarchist Dream Alive. October 1, 2017. Available from: https://www.coindesk.com/guns-crypto-bitcoin-helping-keep-cody-wilsons-anarchist-dream-alive/

[4] Kim T. Seth Klarman Calls Bitcoin a 'Trading Sardine,' Others Say 'Speculative Mania'—They are Right. CNBC. December 15, 2017. Available from: https://www.cnbc.com/2017/12/15/seth-klarman-calls-bitcoin-a-trading-sardine-others-say-speculative-mania--they-are-right.html

[5] Torres C. Yellen Says Bitcoin Is a 'Highly Speculative Asset'. Bloomberg Technology. December 13, 2017. Available from: https://www.bloomberg.com/news/articles/2017-12-13/yellen-says-cryptocurrency-bitcoin-is-highly-speculative-asset

[6] Gil-Pulgar J. Former Chairman of the U.S. Federal Reserve Alan Greenspan argues: Bitcoin is not rational. Bitcoin News. December 8, 2017. Available from: http://bitcoinist.com/greenspan-declares-bitcoin-irrational/

[7] Pollock D. Billionaire Investor Warns Bitcoin is Pyramid Scheme. Cointelegraph. July 27, 2017. Available from: https://cointelegraph.com/news/billionaire-investor-warns-bitcoin-is-pyramid-scheme

[8] Lovelace B Jr. Warren Buffett Watcher Echoes Warning on Bitcoin: We're Probably near the Top of a bubble. CNBC. January 11, 2018. Available from: https://www.cnbc.com/2018/01/11/warren-buffett-watcher-were-near-the-top-of-a-bitcoin-bubble.html

[9] Nullen C. Bitcoin is Worthless, Bubble May Pop Soon, Allianz Global Says. Bloomberg Businesweek. March 14, 2018. Available from: https://www.bloomberg.com/news/articles/2018-03-14/bitcoin-is-worthless-bubble-may-pop-soon-allianz-global-says

[10] North G. Bitcoins: The Second Biggest Ponzi Scheme in History. November 29, 2013. Available from: https://www.garynorth.com/public/11828.cfm

[11] Bennington A. Bitcoin Bear Peter Schiff Doubles Down: Even at $4,000 it's Still a 'Bubble'. Coindesk. August 17, 2017. Available from: https://www.coindesk.com/bitcoin-bear-peter-schiff-doubles-even-4000-still-bubble/

[12] North GI. Broken Pencil: An Economic Analysis of Bitcoins. December 6, 2013. Available from: https://www.garynorth.com/public/11857.cfm

[13] LeRoux C. The Inability of Bitcoin to Serve for Rational Economic Calculation. June 11, 2014. Available from: https://peacefreedomprosperity.com/7776/inability-bitcoin-serve-rational-economic-calculation/

[14] Shostak F. The Bitcoin Money Myth. Mises Institute. April 17, 2013. Available from: https://mises.org/library/bitcoin-money-myth

[15] Graf KS. Bitcoin as Medium of Exchange Now and Unit of Account Later: The Inverse of Koning's Medieval Coins. September 14, 2013. Available from: http://konradsgraf.com/blog1/2013/9/14/bitcoin-as-medium-of-exchange-now-and-unit-of-account-later.html

[16] von Mises L. Human Action: A Treatise on Economics. Scholar's ed. Auburn, AL: Ludwig von Mises Institute; 1940/1998. Available from: http://mises.org/document/3250/Human-Action

[17] Rothbard Murray N. Man, Economy, and State, with Power and Market. Auburn, AL: Mises Institute; 1970. Available from: http://mises.org/document/1082/Man-Economy-and-State-with-Power-and-Market

[18] Herbener JM. The Pure Time-Preference Theory of Interest. Auburn, Alabama: CreateSpace Independent Publishing Platform; 2011

[19] Hayek F. "The 'Paradox' of Saving". Originally Appeared in the Zeitschrift für Nationalökonomie, Bd. I, Heft III, 1929, Under the Title "Gibt es einen Widersinn des Sparens?. The Translation is the Work of Mr. Nicholas Kaldor and Dr. Georg Tugendhat and was First Published in Economica, May, 1931

[20] Bordo MD, Lane JL, Redish A. Good versus bad deflation: Lessons from the gold standard era. NBER (The National Bureau of Economic Research) Working Paper No. 10329; February, 2004. Available from: http://www.nber.org/papers/w10329

[21] Lewis N. Let's Resolve the Gold Standard 'Deflation' Fallacy. Forbes, Economics & Finance. May 21, 2015. Available from: https://www.forbes.com/sites/nathanlewis/2015/11/21/lets-resolve-the-gold-standard-deflation-fallacy/

[22] Karsten J, West DM. Venezuela's "Petro" Undermines other Cryptocurrencies–and International Sanctions. Brookings. March 9, 2018. Available from: https://www.brookings.edu/blog/techtank/2018/03/09/venezuelas-petro-undermines-other-cryptocurrencies-and-international-sanctions/

[23] Hosia H, Perry N. This is the First Country to Adopt a Cryptocurrency as its Official Currency. Time. March 5, 2018. Available from: http://time.com/money/5186316/this-is-the-first-country-to-adopt-a-cryptocurrency-as-its-official-currency/

[24] Althauser J. Race Towards the First 'Crypto-Country' in the World. Cointelegraph. October 13, 2017. Available from: https://cointelegraph.com/news/race-towards-the-first-crypto-country-in-the-world

[25] Foote C, Block W, Crane K, Gray S, et al. Economic policy and prospects in Iraq. The Journal of Economic Perspectives. 2004;**18**(3):47-70

[26] Granot E. Ricardo's law of comparative advantage and the Law of Association: A subjective analysis. In: Economics and Development. Rijeka, Croatia: Intech; 2017. Chapter 3

[27] Kinsella S. Against Intellectual Property. Auburn, AL: Mises Institute; 2008

[28] Sampathkumar M. Bitcoin should be 'Outlawed', says Nobel Prize-Winning The Economist. Independent. November 30, 2017. Available from: https://www.independent.co.uk/news/business/bitcoin-latest-news-outlawed-nobel-prize-winner-joseph-stiglitz-comments-a8083416.html

[29] Smart E. 1% of the Bitcoin Community Controls 99% of Bitcoin Wealth. CCN. May 18, 2015. Available from: https://www.ccn.com/1-bitcoin-community-controls-99-bitcoin-wealth/

[30] John McAfee Ups Bitcoin Target Price to $1 Million by End 2020. Available from: https://www.youtube.com/watch?v=bo9zaBZ1VIo&t=917s

[31] Salerno J. Money, Sound and Unsound. Auburn, Alabama: Mises Institute; 2010

[32] Helfferich EG. Das Geld [English Translation, "Money"]. London: Ernest Benn; 1927

[33] Menger C. Principles of Economics. Auburn, Alabama: The Mises Institute; 2004

[34] von Mises L. The Theory of Money and Credit. New Haven: Yale University Press; 1912/1953. Translated by Batson HE

[35] Graf Konrad S. IN-DEPTH | Bitcoins, the Regression Theorem, and that Curious but Unthreatening Empirical World. February 27, 2013. Available from: http://konradsgraf.com/blog1/2013/2/27/in-depth-bitcoins-the-regression-theorem-and-that-curious-bu.html

[36] Shirriff K. Hidden Surprises in the Bitcoin Blockchain and how they Are Stored: Nelson Mandela, Wikileaks, Photos, and Python Software. Available from: http://www.righto.com/2014/02/ascii-bernanke-wikileaks-photographs.html

Chapter 6

# The Condition of the Cryptocurrency Market and Exchanges in Poland

Ireneusz Miciuła

Additional information is available at the end of the chapter

http://dx.doi.org/10.5772/intechopen.79405

**Abstract**

The development of the cryptocurrency market and the implications for the whole economy and finance for all traders cause a keen interest in this subject. The chapter discusses the functioning of a financial system based on cryptocurrencies and its significance for economies. In this chapter, the development of the global cryptocurrency market was presented and the history of the most popular cryptocurrency, bitcoin, was analyzed. The analysis and the assessment of the state and structure of the Polish cryptocurrencies market were presented on the background of the global cryptocurrency market. Also, we presented the possible development paths for the cryptocurrencies market in Poland and in the world.

**Keywords:** cryptocurrencies, financial innovations, cryptocurrency market, polish market, cryptocurrency exchanges, market regulations for cryptocurrencies

## 1. Introduction

This chapter will include the analysis and the assessment of market developments and cryptocurrency exchanges in Poland, along with the attempt to present the perspectives of development. The evaluation will be made on the background of cryptocurrency world.

Cryptographic currency, popularly known as cryptocurrency, is, in the definition, a distributed accounting system based on cryptography, which stores information about the state of ownership in conventional units. The state of ownership is related to individual system nodes (portfolios) in such a way that only the holder of the corresponding private key would have control over the given portfolio, and it was impossible to issue the same unit twice. The creator of the most popular cryptocurrency defines it as follows: it is an electronic coin as a chain of digital signatures. Each owner transfers the coin to the next by digitally signing a hash of the previous transaction and the public key of the next owner and adding these to the end of the coin. A payee can verify the signatures to verify the chain of ownership, what we see in **Figure 1**. However, the problem of course is that the payee cannot verify that one of the owners did not double-spend the coin. A common solution is to introduce a trusted central authority, or mint, that checks every transaction for double-spending [1].

Current commerce on the Internet has come to rely almost exclusively on financial institutions serving as trusted third parties to process electronic payments. While the system works well enough for most transactions, it still suffers from the inherent weaknesses of the trust-based model because it cannot avoid mediating disputes. Therefore, needed is an electronic payment system based on cryptographic proof instead of trust, allowing any two willing parties to transact directly with each other without the need for a trusted third party [2]. A peer-to-peer version of electronic cash would allow online payments to be sent directly from one party to another without going through a financial institution. Digital signatures provide part of the solution, but the main benefits are lost if a trusted third party is still required to prevent double-spending [1]. The entire system operation cryptocurrency is based on cryptology, the field of knowledge about the transmission of information in a manner protected against unauthorized access [3]. However, this system is also based on trust and institutions certifying the authenticity of even cryptographic keys. On the other hand, the currently operating cryptocurrencies are mostly based on bilateral trust (sellers and investors), and additionally, at the very end, the creators have the ability to manipulate and change

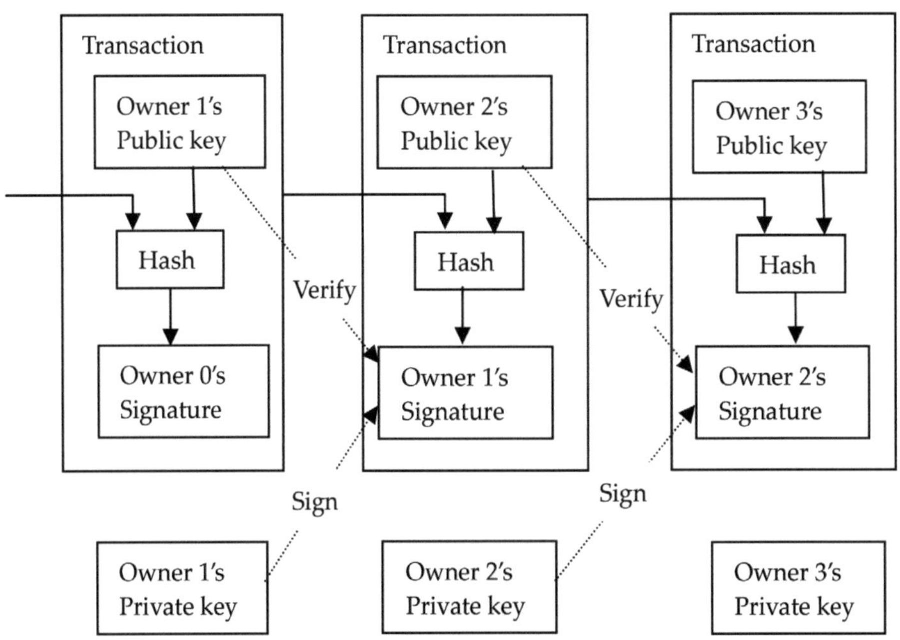


**Figure 1.** Cryptocurrency authentication transaction. Source: own based on: [1].

the operating principles of the algorithms on which the operating system is based. This is the biggest danger, as is evidenced by numerous cryptocurrencies that have gone bankrupt or stopped functioning overnight. That is why this topic is so important. On the one hand, these systems seek solutions that could work without the need for third party trust. The global cryptocurrency system operates despite the lack of confirmation of trust from the countries or institutions. At the same time, it gives the opportunity to speculate and create large estates for private individuals or enterprises, which are basically in the global system unnoticeable to the whole. On the other hand, it can cause great systemic threats and great economic losses around the world and be a source of hiding large crime and financial crises. In this chapter, we will explain how the functioning of cryptocurrency together with the current developments in the world and in this context, analysis and assessment of market cryptocurrency in Poland will be made.

## 2. The current development cryptocurrencies in the world

The biggest interest in cryptocurrencies results from two reasons. First of all, this is due to the idea of freedom and independence from third parties, such as state or financial institutions. Secondly, from the point of view of possible investment gains, both legal and illegal. One of the main features of cryptocurrencies is that it acts like a virtual currency. The holder of such a cryptocurrency stores it on his computer or in a smartphone application in the so-called wallet that only he can access. If he wishes to make a transaction, it takes place electronically, directly between him and the contractor. Each unit of cryptocurrencies has a unique code, which contains information preventing its copying or re-spending. The key to the concept of cryptocurrencies is also the fact that there is no regulator in circulation. Therefore, there is no, for example Central Bank of Crypocurrency, which may decide, for example, to increase the supply of cryptocurrency and thus to decrease its value. The author decides how much of a given cryptocurrency is in circulation at the stage of creating the system. Its value is in the hands of the free market. Trading in cryptocurrencies takes place electronically, without the participation of any banking system directly between users of the cryptocurrency, that is, in peer-to-peer technology. This means that the transaction is not supervised in any way. Therefore, there is no entity that will inform tax authorities if we want to sell a large number of cryptocurrencies, as it happens in the case of banking transactions for an amount exceeding the equivalent of 15,000 Euro. No one can also block our account. The bailiff will not come. Considering the above, it turns out that the mission of cryptocurrency really boils down to one word, which is "freedom." Cryptocurrencies are electronic currencies completely free from the control of politicians, domestic or international financial institutions, whose turnover is not controlled in any way, and is subject only to a strong system of electronic, automated securities.

Cryptocurrencies are, first of all, breakthrough internet technology, and using it as a means of payment is just one of its possible applications. It is a system based on a peer-to-peer network, that is, fully dispersed, without a central unit, organization or place that controls it. System users, their computers, are network nodes through which transactions are exchanged, authorized, and settled. This system stores information on the state of ownership in contractual units of cryptocurrency. The possession of a given cryptocurrency is related to individual portfolios containing information about the cryptocurrency of a given user.

The wallet is created automatically during the first user authorization in the system. Only the owner of the corresponding encrypted private key has control over the portfolio. Advanced mathematical and cryptographic methods make it impossible to double-issue cryptocurrency, counterfeit or theft. The whole system is based on blockchain technology.

Cryptocurrency is the first invention in the financial system that was developed outside of financial institutions, even without cooperation with them. It is innovative, simple, and does not use existing financial systems. Moreover, it poses a threat to the status quo of the financial system. Therefore, many market regulators, including the countries and international financial institutions, regard this system as a threat primarily of their own income and generally understood power and authority. For this reason, we observe a very different reaction of countries in the world.

Starting from Japan (as an example of the most far-reaching regulation), one can point to the rapid evolution of the Japanese regulators' approach. Starting from the recognition of cryptocurrency as a means of payment, but not yet as the currency introduced by the act on payment services of 25 May 2016, until the adoption in April 2018 of new regulations fully recognizing cryptocurrencies as legal tender. What is more, the Japanese Central Bank began work on creating its own digital currency, whose working name is J-Coin. On the other hand, we have a contrast. For example, in China, we have a ban on making cryptocurrencies. On the other hand, Bangladesh and Nepal, by introducing the relevant regulations, penalized the marketing of cryptocurrencies. In Bangladesh, the use of cryptocurrencies is currently regarded as a violation of the provisions on money laundering and is punishable by imprisonment of up to 12 years. In Nepal, after introducing changes prohibiting the circulation of crypts, the first detainees of such activities took place [4]. On the other hand, many countries have no regulations on this matter, and in principle, are considering which party to address in relation to cryptocurrencies. For example, in Europe, so far none of the countries has banned trading in cryptocurrencies. However, many countries are preparing the right law because they are aware of the facts that point to the rapid growth of transactions in cryptocurrencies. Most countries see this as primarily a threat system, which will receive the role of management, which takes obvious opportunity to influence the financial and economic phenomena. Maybe a system in which there is no supervision of specific organizations due to a change in rules it's a good direction of development. However, it is certainly not a cryptocurrency system, where one person can play such a role [5].

Currently, the most popular cryptocurrency in the world is bitcoin. It has the highest market capitalization and the highest rate, and often as part of discussing the topic, cryptocurrencies are a flagship example. The most popular cryptocurrency in the world, bitcoin, was created in 2008. It is not known who are its creators. Almost simultaneously, three IT specialists (King, Oksman, and Bry) patented solutions similar to those on which the bitcoin system was based [6]. So, we see that bitcoin is 10 years old. Due to the review of Bitcoin's development history, you can notice characteristic phases for the entire cryptocurrency market.

- February 9, 2011—for the first time in history, one bitcoin was priced at the same rate as the US dollar.
- April 5, 2011—the Polish bitmarket.eu market is established.
- June 2, 2011—1 BTC was valued at $ 10.
- August 26, 2011—the Polish bitomat.pl. stock market collapsed, with 17,000 BTC lost.
- November 19, 2013—1 BTC was valued at $ 1000.
- February 13, 2012—the collapse of the large TradeHill exchange.
- May 11, 2012—the fall of the Bitcoinica platform.
- July 2013—billionaires Winklevoss brothers are entering Bitcoin.
- March 25, 2013—Denmark exempts bitcoin sales from tax.
- September 20, 2013—Bitcoin recognized as a full-fledged private money in Germany.
- December 5, 2013—beginning of the bitcoin ban in China.
- February 28, 2014—the demise of the largest bitcoin exchange—Mt.Gox.

The first characteristic phase, which is noticeable in the graphs of all new cryptocurrencies, is the so-called the phase of gaining confidence. It is visible on the cryptocurrency charts, which have passed to the following phases: the second (interest, growth) and third (determination of the maximum value for the period). The time between consecutive phases is different for specific cryptocurrencies and depends on many factors. There are many examples of cryptocurrencies that have arisen and fallen in the first phase of the life cycle. There are also many examples, often local cryptocurrencies, which have passed to the third phase, where the achieved maximum value is visible, followed by a very fast drop in value or even a momentary fall and the cryptocurrency ceases to function. We also see this on the example of the most popular cryptocurrency, bitcoin. November 19, 2013 reached its maximum value of $ 1000 after which, among others, also due to the collapse after 3 months of the largest bitcoin exchange. This recession lasted for 2 years, where the value accounted for one-fourth of the maximum value achieved in this period, which can be seen in **Figure 2**. The return to the value of 1000 dollars for one bitcoin was made at the end of 2016, so after 3 years. In addition, the actual revival and return to the maximum value from 2013 took place in 2016. This additionally shows very dynamic movements, both upward and downward, in comparison to the existing system of recognized means of payment. There are many examples where there is not so much interest on the part of investors and co-financing as in the case of bitcoin, which causes bankruptcy of the system and the collapse of these cryptocurrencies. This causes a lot of damage to the trust of the cryptocurrency system and gives arguments to their opponents, which show the use of the system to create financial pyramids and other scams. The same negative consequences for the system are caused by falls of exchanges and cryptocurrency exchange platforms. Although in this case, it often happens that the defenders of the current

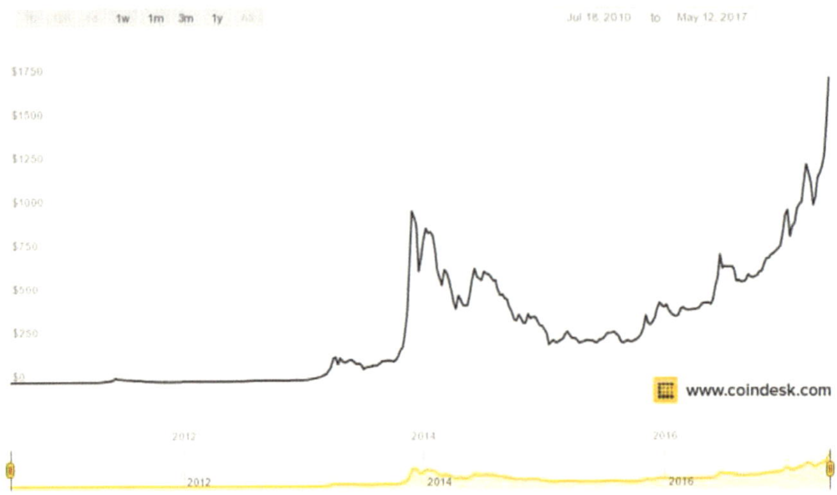


**Figure 2.** Bitcoin exchange rate in the years 2010–2017. Source: [7].

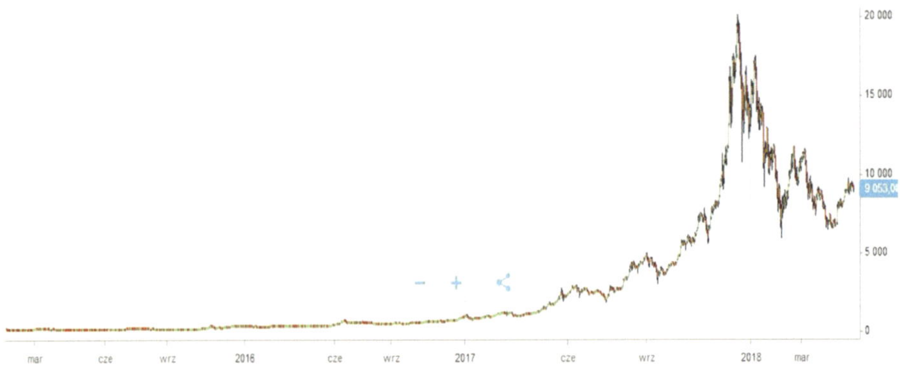


**Figure 3.** Bitcoin exchange rate in the years 2015–2018 (today). Source: [8].

system, that is state and financial institutions, also bear responsibility for these events. For example, additional taxes are imposed in Poland, and financial institutions, such as banks, refuse to provide services to such entities. Analyzing the history of the most popular cryptocurrency, we see that states have different approaches to the cryptocurrency system, from a total ban and establishing penalties to full recognition. Some countries often use the tax burden imposed on cryptocurrencies, but do not intend to lay down specific legal provisions on this matter, although it considers this activity to be legal.

The recent history of Bitcoin, basically from the last year of 2017, shows renewed interest and an almost unimaginable increase in value. From the return and breakthrough value of $ 1000 to as much as $ 20,000 in mid-December 2017 for one bitcoin. Since then, for less than half a year, we have seen a decline in around a quarter of the historical maximum value, another increase and oscillation around half of this value, as shown in **Figure 3**.

- February 20, 2017—you can receive 1055,26 USD for 1 bitcoin.
- March 2, 2017—bitcoin worth more than gold at $ 1268 for 1 BTC.
- December 2017—historical maximum value of 1 bitcoin worth 20,000 dollars.
- May 1, 2018—for 1 bitcoin you can receive 8951.64 USD (31.105 PLN).

Bitcoin is a flagship example of a cryptocurrency system, most of which repeat the regularity of the system's behavior. However, there are several hundred other cryptocurrencies, which are referred to as altcoins (alternative coins, including the "bitherin's younger brother" currency ethereum). The creation of some of them had at the same time to achieve other goals, for example, namecoin creates a decentralized DNS system and peercoin tries to spread the income from the extraction of its units more evenly. There are also plans to build cryptocurrencies on the forecasting market.

New cryptocurrencies are constantly being created due to the use of open source software and P2P networks. The source code is based on free software, so anyone can download it and create your cryptocurrency. Currently, there are more than 1500 individual cryptocurrencies. Many of them work on the same code principle, they present only a few minor changes and different parameters (time distribution of blocks or number of coins) in contrast to the original coin.

Currently, more than 1500 cryptocurrencies are listed on more than 7000 special exchanges market. Each of them has some advantages and unfortunately disadvantages. A large number, especially local cryptocurrencies, have a short history of functioning and then disappear from the market. It has the negative effect of receiving the cryptocurrency system as a whole, because there are many examples for using it for financial fraud purposes. Undoubtedly, however, there are also advantages, the emphasis, and full use of which would require certain legal and technological solutions. To confirm the importance of the subject matter in the world of finance and economies in the world, **Table 1** presents cryptocurrencies, whose market capitalization currently amounts to over 1 billion US dollars.

**Table 1** contains a list of cryptocurrencies with market capitalization exceeding USD 1 billion. Currently, such cryptocurrency is 25. Market capitalization is the value of all coins that are in circulation, multiplied by their current value (Eq. (1)).

$$\text{market capitalization} = \text{number of coins in circulation} \times \text{current value of one coin} \quad (1)$$

The rate defines the price of one digital coin in US dollars. Cryptocurrency is the first invention in the financial system that was developed outside of financial institutions, even without cooperation with them. It is innovative and does not use existing financial systems. Moreover, it poses a threat to the status quo of the financial system. Undoubtedly, this trait of independence and lack of trust in the third party (institutions that create and regulate the financial system) would be a revolution in the world of finance, where only two parties would be required. This is the main argument for creating a system that is not dependent and subjected to the influence of financial regulators. Unfortunately, however, in practice, despite the vision

| No. | Cryptocurrency | Code | Exchange rate | Number of coins | Market capitalization |
|---|---|---|---|---|---|
| 1. | Bitcoin | BTC | $ 8951.6394 | 17,180,188 | $ 153,790,855,757 |
| 2. | Ethereum | ETH | $ 646.5789 | 100,154,753 | $ 64,757,950,249 |
| 3. | Ripple | XRP | $ 0.80371665 | 39,541,619,593 | $ 31,780,258,035 |
| 4. | Bitcoin Cash | XBC | $ 1281.7728 | 17,275,946 | $ 22,143,838,920 |
| 5. | EOS | EOS | $ 16.7904 | 835,329,772 | $ 14,025,521,010 |
| 6. | Cardano | ADA | $ 0.3254823 | 26,188,960,137 | $ 8,524,042,980 |
| 7. | Litecoin | LTC | $ 143.9658 | 56,898,395 | $ 8,191,423,098 |
| 8. | Stellar Lumes | XLM | $ 0.39935016 | 18,759,309,869 | $ 7,491,533,398 |
| 9. | Tronix | TRX | $ 0.09088398 | 66,412,089,292 | $ 6,035,794,995 |
| 10. | NEO | NEO | $ 80.4078 | 65,659,718 | $ 5,279,553,500 |
| 11. | IOTA | IOT | $ 1.8513 | 2,800,940,157 | $ 5,185,380,514 |
| 12. | Monero | XMR | $ 230.3433 | 16,146,465 | $ 3,719,230,081 |
| 13. | Dash | DASH | $ 454.2615 | 8,121,006 | $ 3,689,060,743 |
| 14. | Nem | XEM | $ 0.39074508 | 9,090,909,088 | $ 3,552,227,999 |
| 15. | Tether | USDT | $ 0.99 | 2,450,101,824 | $ 2,425,600,806 |
| 16. | Vechain | VEN | $ 4.3362 | 530,773,566 | $ 2,301,540,339 |
| 17. | Etherum Classic | ETC | $ 20.7207 | 102,514,915 | $ 2,124,180,807 |
| 18. | Qtum | QTUM | $ 21.4731 | 89,476,920 | $ 1,921,346,857 |
| 19. | OmiseGO | OMG | $ 16.1964 | 103,074,544 | $ 1,669,436,555 |
| 20. | Binance Coin | BNB | $ 13.7511 | 115,221,419 | $ 1,584,421,260 |
| 21. | Lisk | LSK | $ 12.2463 | 106,472,521 | $ 1,303,894,445 |
| 22. | RaiBlocks | XRB | $ 9.4347 | 134,639,002 | $ 1,270,278,593 |
| 23. | Bitcoin Gold | BTG | $ 69.7455 | 17,146,505 | $ 1,195,891,577 |
| 24. | Verge | XVG | $ 0.07307982 | 15,092,890,527 | $ 1,102,985,723 |
| 25. | Zcash | ZEC | $ 272.6064 | 3,856,723 | $ 1,051,367,505 |

Source: own study based on the courses of 01/05/2018.

**Table 1.** A list of cryptocurrencies with market capitalization of over USD 1 billion.

of the scattering of the system and dependence only on the parties to the transaction, so it does not work. In fact, a technology-based system also has regulators and is based on trust, but this can be a natural feature of social systems that must be based on social recognition. However, unfortunately many cryptocurrencies and exchange market depend on a group of people or even one person, who may have malicious intentions, as exemplified by many scams related to the cryptocurrency market. On the one hand, manipulations are made by the creators or regulators of the rules of operation, including changes in the algorithm itself, and

http://dx.doi.org/10.5772/intechopen.79405

on the other, players who have a huge impact on the entire market. An excellent example is the most popular cryptocurrency (bitcoin), where 97% of the currency is in the hands of only 4% of all portfolios [9]. Therefore, more and more people and institutions from the financial world warn against investing in cryptocurrencies, speaking about the financial pyramid, the speculative bubble, or ordinary scams. Currently, when they do not function as legal means of payment, it is a form of speculation or thesaurisation of values. However, undoubtedly this technology has great possibilities, which is why it is so difficult to define a system that would function in a safe way. You can store any type of transaction in transaction books. It does not matter if bitcoin represents currency, property, real estate, or shares. Users can decide themselves by defining the bitcoin parameters, which the given bitcoin unit represents. Each bitcoin is individually identifiable and programmable. This means that users can assign different properties to each individual. The user, using specialized applications, can program bitcoin to represent eurocents, company shares, kilowatt hours of energy, votes in elections, loans, or digital holding certificates. Because of this, this cryptocurrency is much more than just money and payments. Bitcoin behavior rules can also be programmed as needed. They can be automatically deleted after the expiration date and can be exchanged; they can automatically return to the owner, if the recipient does not meet, for example, the agreed terms of the transaction, will not pay on time or will not send the goods to the buyer. Just this feature could be used against fraudsters. However, establishing such a system is in fact not an easy task and undoubtedly requires a trusted party, otherwise regulators, who will somehow watch over the safety of turnover. It seems that a financial system based on the discussed technology should go this way. Currently, despite the great interest, the problem itself is not fully recognized as evidenced by, for example, different approaches of countries around the world to properly apply this technology. In the next section, we will look at the development of cryptocurrencies and their exchange market in Poland against the background discussed cryptocurrency market in the world.

## 3. The condition of the cryptocurrency market and exchanges in Poland

Undoubtedly, the development of the cryptocurrency market in a given country depends on government legal decisions in relation to this market. As discussed before, the possibilities are a lot, from a total ban to full acceptance as a full-fledged currency, and there are many important options and solutions. At present, Poland has taken 24th place on the list of countries through which the largest cryptocurrencies take place. Of course, this also has to do with the state's decisions in relation to the cryptocurrency market.

Currently in Poland, cryptocurrencies are not considered a currency unit, a payment instrument, or electronic money. However, in spite of this, creating units as part of the built-in algorithm (so-called mining or digging) is legal under the law. However, as a result, it often happens that cryptocurrencies do not benefit from the tax relief provided for currency trading. In any case, the impression is often that, just like in Poland, states deliberately impose tax burdens, on the one hand, for profitable purposes for the state budget, and on the other hand, for the purpose of authenticating and protecting potential clients. The Commission on Financial Supervision (KNF) and the National Bank of Poland (NBP) also launched a campaign on this subject. They remind about the risk associated with investing in cryptocurrencies and issuing an official warning, where they pay attention to the possibility of theft, high price volatility, and the lack of any guarantee of invested capital.

In tax matters, many countries see short-sightedly only the desire to tax for profit. In addition, disinformation and lack of regulation occur in many countries. However, even without such regulations, tax officials collect data on the circulation of cryptocurrencies and in order to show income in testimony and pay tax. Therefore, the taxation of trading in cryptocurrencies raises a number of controversies on the basis of tax law due to the lack of detailed regulations relating to these issues. It can be safely said that this is one of those examples where legal regulations, including tax regulations, do not keep up with the economic reality. In addition, on April 20, 2018 in Poland, there was a protest against the unclear introduction of tax obligations in relation to trading in cryptocurrencies. The regulators themselves did not understand the clarity of the cryptocurrency market and introduced defective legal provisions. At present, in Poland in the area of personal income tax, the income from the sale of purchased cryptocurrencies will constitute income from property rights referred to in the abovementioned Art. 18 of the act on personal income tax [10].

The consequence of obtaining income from property rights is an obligation on the seller to prove this income and to calculate the tax due on the sum of income obtained according to the tax scale. However, during the tax year, there is no obligation to pay advance payments for personal income tax. On the other hand, with regard to VAT, the turning point in the tax authorities' approach to taxation with this trade tax was the judgment of the Court of Justice of the European Union (CJEU) in the Skatteverket/David Hedqvist case, in which the CJEU stated that the exemption from VAT provided for in Art. 135 of law 1e) [11]. The VAT Directive also covers the provision of services consisting in the exchange of traditional currencies into units of virtual currency, and vice versa, made on payment of an amount corresponding to the margin resulting from the difference between the price at which the trader acquires currencies and the price at which he sells them to clients. The above position of the CJEU is currently applied by tax authorities, who previously refused to apply exemption to this type of services. In current interpretations, tax authorities take the view that the cessation of the use of Art. 43 section 1 point 7 of the act on goods and services tax relating to transactions in currencies, banknotes, and coins used as legal tender [12].

The KNF wants to clearly separate the topic of cryptocurrencies and new financial technologies. We are positive about new technologies in the financial market. When it comes to blockchain technology, we support it and see it as a chance for development, so it is not like crypts and blockchain have to be put in one bag. The KNF explains that the first step was the Anti-Money Laundering and Terrorism Financing Act. In his opinion, however, there are still no mechanisms to protect cryptocurrencies from dishonest sellers. It is an unregulated market, so there are no tools to protect consumers. At the time when such an entity would cease its activity from day to day, the institutions are not able to help clients to recover their funds. Undoubtedly, there is an unfavorable regulatory and tax climate in Poland, as well as information chaos, which limits the use of cryptocurrencies. In addition, four banks (BZ WBK, mBank, PKO BP, and Alior Bank) terminated contracts with companies that ran platforms allowing them to invest in cryptocurrencies. As a result of such actions, the largest stock exchange of cryptocurrencies in Poland announced that they are considering relocating their activities abroad. **Table 2** presents the largest stock exchange of cryptocurrencies operating in Poland.

Percentage share in 2017 of the listed cryptocurrency exchanges in Poland was as follows: BitBay (49%), Bitmarket.pl. (28%), Coinroom (16%), Nevbit (4%), and Bitmachin (3%). Daily turnover on the cryptocurrency market in Poland reached PLN 50 million in 2017. According to Morgan Stanley, most of the registered cryptocurrency exchanges are in the UK [14].

The creator of the first Polish coin was at the beginning of January 2014 "djbartek"—author of Dubstepcoin (abbreviation: WUBS). His coin referred to the popular genre of electronic music—dubstep—and had the chance to get something from this popularity. She did not make it because she fell. However, he is about to make his debut again, but currently it is only plans. Therefore, taking into account the currently existing cryptocurrencies, the first three Polish cryptocurrencies, which were created at the beginning of 2014, include:

1. PolCoin (PLC), is the first Polish virtual currency. Established in January 2014 as a clone gaining Bitcoin popularity. It is based on the same SHA256d algorithm. Currently, it is a completely Polish project in which only the Polish team of creators and Polish capital are involved. Currently, it is being developed by the third team of developers. The reborn Polcoin project is based on a new block chain. Polcoin has a stable network of nodes and developers are working on its development. The main assumption, like other world cryptocurrencies, is the release from the bondage of banks. According to the assumptions, the value of Polcoina should grow in the long-term perspective due to the rigid limitation of supply embedded in the system while increasing demand. An additional reason for increasing the rate of increase in the value of the currency is the growing awareness of the widely understood cryptocurrencies and their usefulness. The history of transactions between addresses is public and available to anyone, when the assumptions of the Satoshi Nakamoto manifesto are guaranteed, the far-reaching anonymity of the transaction is guaranteed by the inability to explicitly state, who is the holder of the given address. This is the first and one of the major differences compared to banking systems in which transaction logs are one of the most watched types of registers. Polcoin is above the state, it is not issued by an organ connected with any state administration, and the auditor is the Polcoina community. It is already used as a means of payment. At present, you can pay with Polcoin, among others, in one stationary store and several online stores [15].

2. PolishCoin (PCC)—created to help Polish people in making the first step in the world of digital money. In terms of new technologies, access to them, and even awareness of their existence, Poland is at the back of the world and Europe. That is why we created PolishCoin (PCC). Experts believe that so far, it is the best prepared cryptocurrency from Poland and is available on one of the exchange cryptocurrency exchanges. Ultimately, the creators want to disseminate PolishCoin enough to hit the global cryptocurrency exchanges.

| | BitBay | BitMaszyna | Coinroom | NevBit | BitMarket.pl |
|---|---|---|---|---|---|
| Company's headquarters (address) | BitBay Sp. z o.o. st. Zacisze 2/6, 40–025 Katowice | Androbayt Sp. z o.o. st. Słowackiego 12, 87–800 Włocławek | Coinroom Sp. z o.o. st. Janka Muzykanta 60 02–188 Warsaw | Nevonet Sp. z o.o. st. Kołłątaja 47/43 81–333 Gdynia | Michau Enterprises Limited Chytron 26, Office 21 1075 Nikozja Cypr |
| Registered Capital | 100,000 PLN | 50,000 PLN | 100,000 PLN | 10,000 PLN | — |
| Available cryptocurrencies | BTC, LTC, ETH, XRP, XBC, DASH, LSK, BTG | BTC, LTC, LSK, DOGE, KBM | BTC, LTC, ETH, DASH, XMR, BCC, PIVX, ZCOIN, LSK, ZEC, ETC, VTC ZOI, HUSH | BTC, LTC | BTC, LTC, PPC, DOGE, XRP, BTG |
| Available currencies | PLN, USD, EUR | PLN | PLN, USD, EUR, GBP, NOK, CHF, CZK, DKK | PLN | PLN, EUR |
| Commissions on transactions | 0.43–0.25% | 0% | 0.39–0.15% | 0% | 0.00–0.45% |
| Commissions on deposits/withdrawals in PLN | 0/1 PLN—simple transfer, 10 PLN—fast transfer 10-20PLN—withdrawal from an ATM | 0 (Simple transfer), 1.9% (Pay By Link)/1 PLN (simple transfer), 10 PLN (fast transfer) | 0 (Simple transfer), 2% (dotpay)/1 PLN (for PLN, USD, EUR—simple transfer) | 0/1 PLN | 0/1 PLN—simple transfer, 0.95% payment amounts—fast transfer, 10-20PLN—withdrawal from an ATM |
| Commissions on deposits/withdrawals in BTC | 0 BTC/0.0002 BTC | brak/0.0001 BTC | brak/0.0001 BTC | brak/0.0001 BTC | brak/0.0001 BTC |
| The minimum number of BTC confirmations | 3 | 3 | 3 | 6 | 3 |
| The minimum value of the offer (purchase/ sale) of BTC | 5 PLN | 10 PLN | debt: 1 crypto: 0.001 | 0.01 BTC | 0.01/0.01 |
| The minimum withdrawal amount (PLN \ BTC) | 5 PLN/0.001 BTC | Greater than fees/BTC without limits | Greater than fees/BTC without limits | 10 PLN/0,0002 BTC | 10/0.01 |
| Lever | — | — | — | — | Lever + Swap |

http://dx.doi.org/10.5772/intechopen.79405

| | BitBay | BitMaszyna | Coinroom | NevBit | BitMarket.pl |
|---|---|---|---|---|---|
| Payment methods | Simple transfer, fast (express) transfer, payment by InPost money transfer, withdrawal at an ATM | Simple transfer, fast transfer | Simple transfer, fast transfer | Simple transfer | Simple transfer, BlueCash |
| Two-factor authentication | Token SMS, Rublon or Google Authenticator | TAK (2FA) | Google Authenticator | — | TAK (2FA) |
| Requirement of verification | After exceeding 15,000 euros payments per account per year | Trade | Payment of fiats | Payment of fiats | After exceeding 1000 euro payments to the account |
| Verification method | Scan/photo of the identity document | Execution of a bank transfer to a designated account | Supply from your bank account with any amount or scan of your ID | Supplying from your bank account with any amount | transfer from a Polish bank account and sending a code to the address of the registrant or scan identity document |
| Limitations of an unverified user | Not to exceed the amount of payments/above 15,000 EUR per year | Blocked: deposit/ withdrawal of funds-trade | Blocked: payments of classic currencies | Blocked: payments of classic currencies | Blocked: withdrawal from the account—account closure |
| The duration of the verification process | Up to 12 hours | Up to 24 hours | Up to 48 hours | — | Up to 48 hours |

Source: [12, 13].

**Table 2.** The five largest stock exchange of cryptocurrencies in Poland.

3. PLNcoin (PLNc)—on March 17, 2014, another Polish cryptocurrency started—PLNcoin. The creators of this coin, before the official opening, extracted 2 million coins. They distributed them for free in exchange for setting up an account on their site. 16,000 profiles have been created on their website. The currency appeared on several stock exchanges, and the company organizing foreign travels declared that it respected payments in PLNc next to Bitcoin and Litecoin.

The creators of these Polish cryptocurrencies declare that we have created them in order to be able to pay in the virtual world for what we want and to whom we want without the control of banking institutions or the government [16]. This is the most frequently mentioned argument emphasizing the advantages of developing a new financial system based on cryptocurrencies. Unfortunately, there are also many uncontrolled threats. For example, skeptics indicate that many cryptocurrency writers are trying to use the prevailing socio-economic climate to earn from "pump and dump"—artificial price raising to sell coins or stocks when others are interested in them. They elevate the value of cryptocurrencies without any intention of building new economic infrastructure. Creators of all are dreaming that one day, their coins will become the means of payment. And for people, who decide to dig and collect coins that will make up for the chance to sleep on bitcoin. There is no point in cheating. Most coins will go into nonexistence after few months [17].

In the Polish market cryptocurrency, unfortunately, is dealing with chaos and destruction—in the best Polish execution. The only positive movement in relation to the cryptocurrency market is the issued statement of state authorities that the circulation of cryptocurrencies does not violate national and EU law, but their possession is associated with high risk, although it is definitely too small activity of legislative bodies. On the other hand, on the basis of global events in Poland, we are also moving toward the introduction of cryptocurrencies on certain legal regulations. An example will be new information obligations. The Ministry of Finance wants to cover the information obligation of the company trading in cryptocurrencies, such as bitcoin. The idea was dealt with by members of the Public Finance Committee, who were working on a government bill on counteracting money laundering and financing of terrorism. Currently, the first Polish act on cryptocurrencies awaits the signature of the president. They talked about them and blockchain technologies yesterday, among others experts from the National Bank of Poland and the Polish Financial Supervision Authority. As they said, we will have to wait at least 2 years for a full legal regulation of this issue. This is a good direction that already works, for example, in Japan. Undoubtedly, one should analyze the history of cryptocurrencies in countries that have experience in this sector due to faster development and that can be said for years. Because the collapse of the cryptocurrency exchange market in Japan took place already in 2014 and on these experiences regulations were introduced, which will now be introduced in Poland. It is a pity that it was not done earlier, learning from experience from other markets that already existed. In Poland, history has repeated itself and the regulations introduced are the aftermath of the fall of Bitcurex cryptocurrency in October 2016. Suddenly it was closed, and more than 2000 Bitcoin belonging to users were embezzled. However, as a result of the lack of regulation, no investor or consumer protection institutions have legal assistance options.

## 4. Conclusions

Cryptocurrencies are not controlled by governments or central banks. Countries usually use two tactics. Some adopted the ostrich strategy, hoping that the fashion will pass by itself and generally does not introduce any regulations on this subject, only those that result from the law of the associated countries, that is, refer to, for example, European Union Member States, as in the case of Poland. The other part, however, wants to try and partly take control and earn on it. For example, in Japan, bitcoin has become a fully-fledged payment instrument. However, due to experience (the collapse of the Mt.Gox stock exchange in 2014 and the disappearance of 850,000 bitcoins), the government of Japan has clearly defined regulations. For example, entities that want to run cryptocurrency exchange services must appear in the register of the Financial Services Agency of Japan, which carries out additional supervision.

Countries such as Russia, Ukraine, Belarus, and Lithuania are in favor of earning money. These countries near Poland, due to the restrictions and unclear actions of state authorities, will simply take over cryptocurrency market participants and they will be earning money. On the other hand, the Polish government does not do much as part of real activity. Admittedly, the chaos related to the tax interpretation of the cryptocurrency market has finally been partially resolved, but no doubts have been finally resolved, which has a negative impact on investors. Because the Polish government stated that it is not going to issue a general tax interpretation in this matter. According to analysts, these negligence (lack of legal regulations) and lagging behind simply lose the chance of big money. For example, in 2016, the industry cryptocurrency in Poland paid over PLN 100 million in taxes.

An example is the Auroracoin cryptocurrency (Iceland's national coin) introduced in 2014. During the year, half of all coins were distributed to Iceland's citizens. Everyone is eager (Icelandic population is about 330,000 people), he got 31 coins, worth about 380 dollars. The goal of the creators is to decentralize control over money and revive the local economy, which has long been struggling with the fall in the value of the Icelandic crown. In the coming years, all eyes will look to Iceland. What the Icelanders will do—whether they are interested in the coin and whether they will start trading it—may depend on the future of national crypts in other countries. According to the Wall Street Journal, more than 70 hedge funds are currently investing in cryptocurrencies, and each day, the value of operations carried out with bitcoins reaches 750 million dollars. For the development of the cryptocurrency market, solutions that increase the security of cryptocurrencies will be necessary, which is another fundamental problem to be solved [18].

The most important factors that fundamentally affect the cryptocurrencies include:

1. Confidence of users and investors—cryptocurrencies are virtual money that do not settle in any physical form. Their value is mainly justified by the offer and demand of users [19]. If the demand for cryptocurrencies increases, their exchange rate also increases. Conversely, if people get rid of cryptocurrencies, their exchange rate will decrease.

2. Use of cryptocurrencies—cryptocurrencies were created as a virtual currency for fast and cheap internet transactions. The more vendors support and accept cryptocurrencies, the

more they are used in practice and the greater the user community will be. Due to the long-growing value of cryptocurrencies, they are increasingly used for investment purposes. In countries with an unstable economy, virtual currencies are bought in order to preserve the value of their own money. Some cryptocurrencies (e.g., Ethereum) are also used by the so-called smart contracts. Cryptocurrencies without practical use, sooner or later cease to exist.

3. Intervention of regulatory and supervisory authorities—if the government of an economically significant state starts supporting cryptocurrencies, the trust of users will usually increase, which will also increase the value of this cryptocurrency [20]. For example, when in April 2017, Japan recognized Bitcoin as a legal currency, its value increased significantly. But it works the other way round. Restrictions or bans on cryptocurrencies by state offices may start a sharp drop in the market. For example, in September 2017, China banned cryptocurrencies, which resulted in a fall in the exchange rate. The Bitcoin and cryptocurrency regulations are also prepared by the European Central Bank.

4. Media attention—information about the growing value of cryptocurrencies attracts new investors, which increases demand and the cryptocurrency rate increases. Also, the views of well-known personalities and companies influence price increases or decreases. An example was the opinion of JPMorgan general director, Jamie Dimon, from September 2017, who described Bitcoin as a fraud and said that the owners of bitcoins will suffer great losses in the future. The Bitcoin market reacted to this message with a decline [21].

5. Manipulating courses—investors use a manipulation technique known as "pump and dump." This technique involves the purchase of cryptocurrency for a low rate and its subsequent media propagation. This will attract new investors who will increase the rate. In the case of liquid markets, we can also increase the price by buying currency in large quantities [22]. When people notice that the rate of a given cryptocurrency increases, they will start investing, which will increase it. In the meantime, we can gradually buy a cryptocurrency for a much higher price than the purchase price. Without media propagation and other investors, the cryptocurrency will start to fall, but this does not apply to us because we have already sold the currency. This often also applies to the creators themselves or organizers and managers of many cryptocurrencies, which arise in order to create such a specific pyramid of finance, only for the purposes of their own income. This method (buy cheap—to convince others to buy—expensive to sell), unfortunately, the natural development of cryptocurrencies is not conducive and increases the high volatility of cryptocurrencies.

6. Technological factors (creators, managers, regulators)–a change of course can also be manipulated by changes in the source code, for example, by implementing various improvements or changes in the number of coins available on the market.

7. Organizational factors—for example, factors affecting the extraction of cryptocurrencies (difficulties in mining, or the price of energy, which, as studies in the literature show, reach huge values comparable to the energy needed to satisfy thousands of households) [23].

8. Substitutes—after all, even assets on the stock exchange affect each other, Bitcoin's growing interest is believed by some to fall in gold, etc. Bitcoin's value influences the rates of other cryptocurrencies, which becomes an alternative to other investments or speculation.

The maximum number of bitcoins created by creators is 21 million, and currently over 17 million are in use, so there will certainly be changes in the assumptions and functioning of entire cryptocurrency markets [24]. The most common opinions are that virtual currencies will be a new stage of development or a haven for cheaters. Certain solutions and regulations should be introduced, including possible ones, based on trust in international institutions that will cause a shift in the likelihood of using the possibility of using cryptocurrencies toward the development of the information society, thus limiting the opportunities of fraudsters and other crimes. Therefore, the main conclusion of the analyzes carried out regarding the cryptocurrency markets is that it will undoubtedly be the future of the financial payment system, but certainly not in its current form. Many local markets will repeat the already known cryptocurrency history, many of which will cease to function in a short time, resembling the financial pyramids. Certainly, cryptocurrency markets will develop and limit negative phenomena that affect confidence in the entire market. It is also possible that, as a result of the lack of other solutions, there will be a need to base cryptocurrencies on trust in states or international organizations. One thing is certain, some solutions will go down, and some will go into widespread use, laying the foundations for the digital financial system of the information society.

## Acknowledgements

I would like to thank Professor Leon Dorozik for his support and interest in the subject matter discussed.

## Conflict of interest

"The author declares no conflict of interest."

## Thanks

Many thanks to family.

## Author details

Ireneusz Miciuła

Address all correspondence to: irekmic@wp.pl

University of Szczecin, Faculty of Economics and Management, Institute of Finance, Szczecin, Poland

## References


[1] Satoshi N. Bitcoin: A Peer-To-Peer Electronic Cash System [Internet]. 2008. Available from: http://bitcoin.org/bitcoin.pdf [Accessed: May 01, 2018]

[2] Investopedia. What is a Cryptocurrency [Internet]. 2018. Available from: https://www.investopedia.com/terms/c/cryptocurrency.asp [Accessed: April 25, 2018]

[3] Christin N. Traveling the silk road: A measurement analysis of a large anonymous online marketplace. In: Proceedings of the 22nd International World Wide Web Conference. Rio de Janeiro. Brazil. 13-17 May 2013. pp. 213-224

[4] Abram G, Szymura T. Bitcoin–Still Cryptocurrency or Currency? [Internet]. 2017. Available from: http://www.infor.pl/Bitcoin-jeszcze-kryptowaluta-czy-juz-waluta.html#ftn16 [Accessed: April 22, 2018]

[5] Moneycontrol. Philippines Boxer to Launch his Own Cryptocurrency [Internet]. 2018. Available from: https://www.moneycontrol.com/news/business/cryptocurrency/philippines-boxer -to-launch-his-own-cryptocurrency-2553257.html [Accessed: April 27, 2018]

[6] Rosic A. What is Cryptocurrency: Everything you Need to Know [Internet]. 2018. Available from: https://blockgeeks.com/what-is-cryptocurrency/ [Accessed: May 01, 2018]

[7] Coindesk. Bitcoin (USD) Price [Internet]. 2018. Available from: https://www.coindesk.com/price/ [Accessed: May 02, 2018]

[8] Money [Internet]. 2018. Available from: https://www.money.pl/pieniadze/bitcoin/ [Accessed: April 28, 2018]

[9] Chaparro F. 97 Percent Bitcoin Are Kept in Only 4 Percent all Portfolios [Internet]. 2018. Available from: https://businessinsider.com.pl/finance/kryptowaluty/analiza-credit-suisse/6g9r9zg [Accessed: April 20, 2018]

[10] Ratajczak M. Niecodzienny protest inwestujących w kryptowaluty [Internet]. 2018. Available from: https://www.money.pl/gospodarka/artykul/rozliczenie-kryptowalut-podatki-protest,185,0,2403001.html [Accessed: April 18, 2018]

[11] Tabaka M. Polish Investors Are Plunged into the Chaos of Tax Interpretations Regarding Cryptocurrencies [Internet]. 2018. Available from: https://www.spidersweb.pl/2018/04/chaos-w-rozliczeniach-podatkowych-z-kryptowalut.html [Accessed: April 26, 2018]

[12] Piech K, Kacwin M. The State of the Cryptocurrency Market in Poland and Possible Tax Revenues of the State Budget. Warsaw. 2017. pp. 1-9

[13] Bitcoin.pl The Review of Polish Stock Exchanges for Cryptocurrencies [Internet]. 2018. Available from: http://bitcoin.pl/zestawienie-gield [Accessed: May 02, 2018]

[14] Cryptocurrencies–Whether Investing in Them is Safe? [Internet]. 2018. Available from: https://www.polskieradio.pl/Artykul/2068287,Jak-uregulowac-obrot-kryptowalutami [Accessed: April 30, 2018]

[15] PolCoin. What is PolCoin? [Internet]. 2014. Available from: https://polcoin.pl/ [Accessed: May 03, 2018]

[16] Woźnicki Ł. PolishCoin, PolCoin I PLNc – Three Polish Cryptocurrencies [Internet]. 2018. Available from: http://wyborcza.pl/1,76842,15707096,PolishCoin__PolCoin_i_PLNc_.html [Accessed: April 15, 2018]

[17] Jagiełowicz M. Cryptocurrencies–To Invest or Not? [Internet]. 2018. Available from: https://www.polskieradio.pl/42/273/Artykul/2107569,Kryptowaluty-czy-inwestowanie-w-nie-jest-bezpieczne [Accessed: April 10, 2018]

[18] Extance A. The future of cryptocurrencies: Bitcoin and beyond. [Internet]. 2015. Available from: https://www.nature.com/news/the-future-of-cryptocurrencies-bitcoin-and-beyond-1.18447 [Accessed: June 10, 2018]

[19] Miciuła I. The concept of FTS analysis in forecasting trends of exchange rate changes. Economics and Sociology. 2014;**7**(2):172-182. DOI: 10.14254/2071-789X.2014/7-2/14

[20] Miączyński P. The Government is Beginning to Notice Cryptocurrencies. Economy; 2017. p. 7

[21] Investplus. Cryptocurrencies – Courses. [Internet]. 2018. Available from: https://invest-plus.cz/pl/kryptowaluty-kursy-pln-usd-ranking-kryptowalut/ [Accessed: May 02, 2018]

[22] Miciuła I. Financial innovations on the currency market as new instruments to risk management. Journal of International Studies. 2015;**8**(1):138-149

[23] Luther WJ. Cryptocurrencies, network effects and switching costs. Contemporary Economic Policy. 2016;**34**:553-571

[24] Antonopoulos AM. Mastering Bitcoin. 2nd ed. O'Reilly: Sebastobol; 2015. 263 p